GOTHENBURG GLORY

by Paul Smith

The Press and Journal
EveningExpress

First published in 2008 by
ABERDEEN JOURNALS LTD.
Mastrick, Aberdeen, Scotland AB15 6DF

Copyright © Aberdeen Journals Ltd.

Text © Paul Smith

www.thenewspaperandgiftshop.co.uk

ISBN 1 901300 12 9

Typeset and design by Bruce Robertson,
D.C. Thomson, Dundee

Printed by D.C. Thomson, Dundee

The photographs drawn from Aberdeen Journals archives can be purchased from
The Photosales Department. Tel. 01224 338011,
or by visiting www.ajlphotosales.co.uk

DEDICATION
To Coral, Finlay and Mia

ACKNOWLEDGEMENTS
Thank you to the Dons team of 1983, without them there would have been no glory in Gothenburg on that famous night. Many people made this project a joy to work on, from Susan McKay at Aberdeen Journals for getting it off and running to Thom Cooper for his loving care and attention to the magical photographs which follow and Bob Stewart and Duncan Smith in the Aberdeen Journals library for their expertise and assistance in the research stages. At DC Thomson, Bruce Roberston and Stuart Cameron turned the vision into reality with real passion during the design and print stages. In compiling and writing the book I spoke to more people than I could possibly mention but I thank players such as Willie Miller, Neil Simpson, Peter Weir, and Neale Cooper for their insights as well as Stewart Milne, Paul Lawrie, Richard Gordon, Lord Provost Peter Stephen and council leader Kate Dean for their fantastic recollections of a golden era. Harry Hynds, Harry Barry and Scott Colegate also all opened up their memory banks during the process to give a unique slant on the events of that period while former Press and Journal sports editor Jim Dolan returned to action for a valued and typically witty contribution. Finally, once again my warmest appreciation is reserved for my wife, Coral, and children, Finlay and Mia, for their support, love and laughs throughout the project and the rest of my family for their encouragement from the moment I first began writing.

CONTENTS

INTRODUCTION

ABERDEEN have what money can't buy – a soul, a team spirit built in a family tradition. With those words, Alfredo Di Stefano succinctly summarised everything that was glorious about the David v Goliath act the Dons produced in the Ullevi Stadium on May 11 in 1983 to slay his mighty Real Madrid side.

The Spanish giants were humbled by the skilful, committed and plucky Scottish underdogs and a piece of football history forever belonged to the Pittodrie. With time, the glory of Gothenburg has not faded but matured and aged like a fine wine. The vintage of 83 has grown to be appreciated by a new generation of the Red Army, even those who were not born when Willie Miller held aloft the European Cup Winners' Cup are well versed in all that the occasion meant to their city and their club.

Twenty-five years on it is a time for celebration, a time to remember when Aberdeen Football Club ruled the roost at home and abroad. In 2008 the heroes of the Ullevi are back in the spotlight having been brought back together by the common bond that will never be broken, uniting fans from all corners of the country and beyond.

In 1983 and the years that have followed the story of Gothenburg has been told a thousand times and the momentous goals replayed over and over again. Gothenburg Glory is not just about unearthing some of the hidden stories behind that great day but more about stoking the memories, some which burn bright and others which are little more than flickering embers after quarter of a century.

Scattered throughout the book are the original newspaper reports from 1982 and 1983 which captured the moment in black and white, a lasting reminder of how the run came together and how it was reported at

the time. Those cuttings have been reproduced as they were written all those years ago, giving a wonderful insight not only into the football world of the 1980s but into the media circle too.

The name that rings clear throughout those cuttings is Alastair Macdonald, the Press and Journal reporter who was there every step of the way. The intrepid Macdonald, in his own distinctive style, charted the highs of the most astonishing season Aberdeen football followers have ever seen. Credited by captain Willie Miller as the most honourable and thorough football writer he has encountered in more than three decades in the game, the doyen of Aberdeen sports reporting can still be seen meticulously charting Dons games from his press seat at the rear of the Main Stand many years after his retirement from frontline duty. His dedication to the cause remains unquestionable and his attention to detail during the most memorable period of his career in journalism ensures the finest details of the run to the Ullevi will be passed from generation to generation.

Of course the archive material tells only half of the story and as a journalist and author this book has taken me on a wonderful and unexpected journey, introducing me to individuals who had some intriguing parts to play in the events of a memorable period in Aberdeen's history. From the club's official travel agent to the man who helped orchestrate the St Clair ferry crossing, from the national media figurehead who overcame his greatest phobia to say 'I was there' to the international sports star who savoured his first big occasion as a spectator rather than a competitor.

The process also reacquainted me with some of the men who wore the red with pride that evening, for whom the sense of achievement has grown with each passing year as they pursue their various careers inside and outside of the beautiful game. In 1983 the victory was huge, in 2008 almost incalculable

● Captain Willie Miller holds aloft the cup amid a sea of fans at the Pittodrie homecoming.

as the realisation of just how difficult to repeat the European success will be at any point in the future hits home. Aberdeen remains the last Scottish club to win at the highest level and the only to have two European trophies to their credit.

There was more to Gothenburg than simply the 1982/83 season and in the pages that follow the years of careful planning that went into building the most famous of Dons teams are examined, as is the impressive yet at times controversial career of the manager who masterminded the whole event.

Gothenburg Glory also explores how, and why, the team was dismantled and catches up with the legends of Sweden 25 years on in the various walks of life the revered former players can now be found. The chapters that follow also chart the careers of the squad men who had roles of varying sizes in the amazing story.

Just as the players have moved on and have had to shift with the times, Aberdeen Football Club is a very different animal from the one which flashed its teeth at the cream of continental football and had the biggest names running for cover.

On the pitch, fortunes improved in time for the silver anniversary, with the perfectly timed return to European action and fine Uefa Cup performances, and the green shoots of financial recovery are also evident after a troubled off-field period.

At the height of the Gothenburg success the story was very different, with the club cash rich and out performing the Old Firm in the boardroom as well as on the turf. As Gothenburg Glory reveals, the success of that era led to unprecedented income for the shrewd Dons directors of the time and it was reinvested in an effort to stay ahead of the Scottish competition.

In truth the battle to match the achievements of Sir Alex Ferguson's finest Aberdeen team was never going to be won. Quite simply the Gothenburg greats combined to create a unique unit, the type of side never seen before or since at Pittodrie. It is a team to be treasured and a team, most of all, to be remembered. Through the images, anecdotes and rare archive material that follow those memories are brought back to life to celebrate the significant landmark of the silver anniversary.

PRELIMINARY ROUND: ABERDEEN v SION
AUGUST 18, 1982: ABERDEEN 7, SION 0   SEPTEMBER 1, 1982: SION 1, ABERDEEN 4

A BERDEEN'S comprehensive victory over Sion across two legs gained the club entry into the tournament, having been paired with the Swiss side in the preliminary round of the competition.

Sion were brushed aside with ease but at the time of the draw the Dons did not anticipate such an easy ride. Although little was known about the club Alex Ferguson's men would face, they had won a place in Europe by beating the more familiar Basle 1-0 in Switzerland's national cup final the previous term. It was their second domestic success in the space of two years, although only the fourth in their history, and attracted 20,000 Sion fans to Berne for the final.

we are not a physical side. my team want to come to Aberdeen to play football

Their hopes of upsetting the Pittodrie side were dealt a blow leading up to the two ties when captain and main striker Jean-Paul Brigger was transferred to Servette in the build-up. He had topped the club's scoring chart with 15 strikes the previous season and had broken into the Swiss national team.

It left Sion with just one full international in their squad in the shape of ageing defender Jean-Yves Valentini, who had moved in the opposite direction from Servette.

The Dons were meticulous in their approach to the tie despite their billing as favourites, with assistant manager Archie Knox sent to the continent to watch their opponents open their league campaign against Aaruu.

Speaking before the first leg, Alex Ferguson said: "They are a very experienced team, with probably only one player under 25. You could not really compare their style of play to any Scottish team as they play a different type of football. They are a better side than the Romanians, Arges Pitesti, we played last season but not in the same class as Ipswich or Hamburg."

Sion manager Leon Walker observed: "We are not a physical side. My team want to come to Aberdeen to play football and show the Scottish fans our natural game. If Aberdeen are very strong and in their best form then they may press us into defence - but if we have the chance, it might be Aberdeen who will have to defend. We do not have the experience Aberdeen have of playing in Europe and we know it will be difficult for us in Scotland."

Although an unknown quantity back in the 1980s, the club, founded in 1909, has gone from strength to strength since its humiliation at the hands of Dons.

They have gone on to win the Swiss cup a further six times and have been crowned champions of the country twice, first in 1992 and then again five years later, on their way to further adventures in European football.

Sion are still based at the Stade Tourbillon but it has changed since the visit from the Dons. The stadium, originally built in the 1960s, was refurbished seven years after Aberdeen's match there and today boasts a capacity in excess of 20,000 in contrast to the 13,000 limit for the 1982 European match.

● Gordon Strachan hammers home the second goal against Sion in the 7-0 win at Pittodrie.

GOAL-HAPPY ABERDEEN MAKE SWISS ROLL!

ABERDEEN	7
FC SION	0

ABERDEEN booked themselves a first round tie against Dinamo Tirana of Albania in the European Cup Winners' Cup when an overwhelming victory over Sion at Pittodrie last night made the second leg of their preliminary round tie in Switzerland next month little more than a formality.

Putting the Swiss part-timers under pressure from the opening minute the Dons found goal scoring relatively easy and on this occasion there was none of the relaxation which cost the Pittodrie side so dearly against SV Hamburg last season.

The controversial four-step carrying rule played a prominent part in the Dons opening goal only two minutes after the kick-off and Eric Black's early counter was followed by goals from Gordon Strachan, John Hewitt and Neil Simpson before the interval.

Sion attempted to halt the goal rush by employing an offside trap after the interval but this

● Neil Simpson clips the ball home to make it 4-0.

● *By Alastair Macdonald*

did not prevent a further three goals from a rampant Aberdeen side. The first of these was contributed by Swiss defender Alain Balet and Mark McGhee and Stuart Kennedy provided the others.

The Dons were so much in command of the game that manager Ferguson took the opportunity to give Peter Weir a run in the final 15 minutes. Weir replaced Black.

This was the type of display t rouse a 13,000 crowd and th spread of the goal-scorin honours is an encouraging sig for the new season.

THERE was enough drama the opening two minutes to la the whole of many another gam It started in 50 seconds when B intercepted a square pass fro Czernicky and broke through his own. The Aberdeen play tried to slide the ball und Pittier's body as the keeper ca out to challenge but the Sw keeper managed to deflect t

...not into the side netting.

...minute later Pittier was again ...volved in the action, this time ...ast as villain, when he broke the ...our-step carrying rule and ...berdeen were awarded an ...direct free-kick just inside the ...ox.

...fter a false start while the ...eferee waved away encroaching ...wiss defenders, Strachan sent ...he free-kick to Simpson whose ...hot was deflected into the air for ...LACK to head goalwards. ...ittier seemed to have the ball in ...is hands but it squirmed from ...is grasp and over the line.

...berdeen might have been ...warded a penalty in 11 minutes ...hen McLeish seemed to be ...ushed by Valentini as he went ...or a Strachan free-kick.

...ion's first attack in 16 minutes ...nded with Bregy shooting wide. ...ittier again broke the four-step ...ule a minute later. This time ...McMaster touched the free-kick ...o Strachan whose flighted lob ...was wide of target.

...A goal, however, was only ...delayed and it came in 21 ...minutes when STRACHAN ...dispossessed Bregy about 25 ...yards from goal, moved into the ...box and beat the advancing ...Pittier with an angled shot.

...A minute later the Dons were ...three ahead. Black just failed to ...connect with a McGhee cross ...from the right but HEWITT, ...coming in from the left wing, ...slammed the ball into the net. ...Aberdeen's continued pressure

● Mark McGhee knocks home the sixth goal

brought a fourth goal in 34 minutes. SIMPSON had a shot blocked but he gathered the rebound, made room for himself by darting to his right and he completed a fine individual effort by beating Pittier with a right foot shot.

Leighton had his first real test of the game in 37 minutes when Luisier sent in a 30-yard shot which the Aberdeen keeper saved. Richard was booked when he impeded McGhee in 49 minutes.

The Dons increased their lead to five in 56 minutes. Under pressure from Black, BALET turned the ball past his own keeper from a Hewitt cross. It seemed an own goal but Black deserved his team-mates' congratulations for his contribution.

Aberdeen then substituted Rougvie for Bell and the goal

procession continued in 62 minutes. McLeish met a Strachan flag kick beyond the far post and headed the ball back across the goalmouth where Black connected with a diving header. The ball came back off the base of the upright and McGHEE side-footed it into the net.

Rougvie had the ball in the Swiss net a minute later but the whistle had gone for an earlier infringement. A Sion raid in 71 minutes saw the Swiss awarded a free-kick on the edge of the Aberdeen penalty box. Bregy sent a low shot across the goalmouth and the ball reached Cucinotta beyond the far post but McLeish made a timely interception at the expense of a corner.

Aberdeen introduced Weir as a substitute for Black in 73 minutes.

With Sion appealing for off-side, KENNEDY broke through for the Dons from a Hewitt pass in 81 minutes and ended his run by scoring goal No.7.

ABERDEEN - Leighton, Kennedy, McMaster, Simpson, McLeish, Miller, Strachan, Black (Weir), McGhee, Bell (Rougvie), Hewitt.

FC SION - Pittier, J. Valentini, P. Valentini, Balet, Richard, Lopez, Bregy, Luisier (Cucinotta), B. Karlen, Cina, Czernicky.

Referee - K. H. Tritschier, West Germany.

BIG WIN DELIGHTS DONS MANAGER

LAST night's victory was the Dons' widest-margin win in any of the three European cup competitions since, in their debut in Europe in 1967, they beat KR Reykjavik 10-0 at Pittodrie in the first leg of a Cup Winners Cup first round tie, following it up with a 4-1 win in Iceland in the second leg for a 14-1 aggregate.

Delighted with a win which removes pressure for the return leg in Switzerland in a fortnight's time, Aberdeen manager Alex Ferguson said: "The second leg is now a bonus for us in that it gives me more freedom to choose a team for the occasion. I may use the game to introduce a younger player to European football or rest some of my regulars for the opening Premier Division game against Dundee United on the following Saturday.

"We must now aim to take a similar advantage of playing the first leg at home when we meet Dinamo Tirana in the first round."

Sion officials might not have expected anything better than a draw at Pittodrie, but the extent of their defeat came as a bitter disappointment.

The Dons' only casualty was Mark McGhee, who took an ankle knock, but he is expected to be fit for Saturday.

● Mark McGhee looks on as Sion defender
Balet turns the ball past his helpless goalkeeper

● The six Dons goalscorers face the camera after the 7-0 win against Sion. From left, back row: Mark McGhee, John Hewitt, Neil Simpson. Middle: Eric Black, Stuart Kennedy. Front: Gordon Strachan.

ABERDEEN COMPLETE EURO MISSION

● Alastair Macdonald reports from Switzerland

FC SION	**1**
ABERDEEN	**4**
(Aggregate 1-11)	

THE Dons duly completed the annihilation of Sion in the Tourbillon Stadium last night to clinch a first round meeting with Dinamo Tirana, of Albania, in the European Cup Winners' Cup.

The Swiss side turned in a much better performance than they did in the fist leg at Pittodrie, but they were no match for the Dons, who left it to the second half before turning the screw on their Swiss opponents.

The all-seated stadium was only sparsely populated with a 2,400 crowd, but many of the Swiss fans stayed to give the Aberdeen side a generous round of applause after the final whistle.

The Dons suffered a first half setback when, immediately after taking the lead through John Hewitt, Sion struck back to equalise within a minute.

● Mark McGhee in full flight against Sion in Switzerland.

That, however, was the home side's last piece of success as the Dons pressed home their technical superiority with three second half goals from Willie Miller and Mark McGhee (2).

During the first half Sion tried to contain the Scots by operating an offside trap, and three of the four "goals" which Aberdeen had disallowed in the opening 45 minutes were for offside.

A bonus for Aberdeen was that the injured Alex McLeish made a half hour appearance as a substitute. Operating in a midfield role, he came through this test with no apparent trouble and should be fit to resume against Dundee United at Tannadice on Saturday.

A second piece of good news for the Dons was that at home in Scotland Dundee drew with Morton to give Aberdeen a place in the quarter-final of the League Cup.

HOW THE TEAM WAS BUILT

ALEX FERGUSON is the man who built the team, the master of the managerial craft who moulded the Aberdeen side which made history in Gothenburg, but he was not the only coach to claim an influence on the class of 1983. The team that shocked Real Madrid was a full decade in the making, with a succession of managers helping to shape the blocks that fitted together to form the most successful side in the club's illustrious history.

The process began in 1973 during Jimmy Bonthrone's tenure in the Pittodrie manager's chair. It was Bonthrone who set in place the foundation of the monumental team when he installed Willie Miller, captain in waiting, as the rock at the heart of Aberdeen's side. Miller was the first of the heroes from the Ullevi to be introduced to the Red Army, appearing in the final game of the 1972/73 season in a 2-1 league win at Morton.

He had arrived far earlier, plucked from Glasgow schools football at the start of the 1970s, just 15 when he first represented the Dons in a local youth tournament. Miller was persuaded to sign as a professional at Pittodrie and learnt his trade as a prolific striker on loan with Peterhead and under Teddy Scott's wing in the reserves. It was Scott who turned to the forward as an emergency sweeper and launched one of Scotland's most distinguished defensive careers by chance, calling on Miller to switch to the back four after Ian Hair had suffered an injury.

His first game for the reserves in his new position was against Rangers and he stole the show, leading Bonthrone to agree to Scott's suggestion that they should keep Miller at the back. The rest, as they say, is history. He was 17 when he made his first team debut, just 20 when he lifted his first trophy as captain of the side in 1976 and still only 28 when he steered his side to the European Cup Winners' Cup.

Miller was a 15 year-old centre forward with Glasgow side Eastercraigs when he signed for the Dons, fresh from his juvenile outfit's triumph in the under-16 Scottish Amateur Cup. They defeated Celtic Boys Club 4-2 in the final, Miller grabbed a double and was denied a hat-trick by the crossbar – having scored all five goals in his side's 5-0 victory agains Possil in the semi-final of the national competition.

Eastercraigs secretary Ian Stevenson said: "The Dons are calling him up for the start of next season and I think he will be a revelation. He is a natural footballer and has an ideal build."

Bristol City and Bury both took the promising Glaswegian south for trials but it was Aberdeen chief scout Bobby Calder, acting on advice from his Dons scouting colleague Jimmy Carswell, who won the race. He turned up at the Miller household with chocolates for the player's mother, cigarettes for his father and sweets for the children. Miller was recruited and travelled north during school holidays for training sessions, signing under the watchful eye of legendary manager Eddie Turnbull just a month before the coach departed for Hibs and Bonthrone took over. Miller had played for both the Glasgow and Scottish school select teams - as a goalkeeper for his city side at primary school age, before turning goalscorer. He hit 22 goals as an attacker for Peterhead in the Highland League

he hit 22 goals as an attacker for Peterhead in the Highland League

before his conversion to defence at the end of his loan spell with the Blue Toon.

John McMaster was another Bonthrone protege who survived the relatively lean 1970s to savour the Ferguson glory days. Born in Greenock just 10 weeks before Miller, he was another teenage recruit at Pittodrie and part of a reserve league winning side featuring Miller, Ian Hair, Ian Purdie, Chic McLelland and Duncan Davidson. He was another of the youngsters sent out to the Highland League to toughen up, spending a period on loan at Peterhead after signing from junior outfit Port Glasgow as a 17 year-old.

Mc Master had to wait just a little longer than Miller for his first taste of first team action, making his debut at the start of the 1974/75 season, but the versatile and skilful left sided performer became an integral part of the side under a succession of managers. His career was almost cut short in 1980 when he suffered a serious knee injury in a European Cup tie against Liverpool but he defied medical opinion to recover and regain his place in Ferguson's plans.

McMaster first caught the attention of Aberdeen scout Bobby Calder while turning out for Port Glasgow Rovers, champions of the Paisley and District Under Age League, in 1971. He shone in a Dons trial match against East Fife the following year, alongside Rovers team-mate Bobby Street, and both youngsters were signed.
McMaster, a 16 year-old left winger, made his reserve team debut just 10 days after moving to the club and the following season was loaned to the Blue Toon.

He scored two goals for the Buchan side in a 2-2 draw against the Dons in a friendly towards the end of that campaign, having also scored a double for the Highland League side in a 2-1 win against the Pittodrie reserves weeks earlier, and that form persuaded Aberdeen to recall him immediately.

After falling out of the first team picture in 1977 McMaster attracted the interest of Ayr United but chose to stay and fight for his place, a wise decision as the champagne era began.

Bonthrone's third and final contribution to the Gothenburg side was Doug Rougvie. The big Fifer was spotted playing juvenile football on his home patch but lured north by Aberdeen and followed the well trodden path to the Highland League, farmed out to Keith and winning a Highland League Cup winner's medal with the Maroons during his stint at Kynoch Park.

Born in Ballingry in May 1956, Rougvie signed for the Dons in 1972 and waited patiently for three years for his debut. It came when Bonthrone pitched him in against Celtic in a League Cup tie his side lost 1-0 and he continued to dip in and out of the team under Ally MacLeod and Billy McNeill until Alex Ferguson arrived and installed him as a key man in his Aberdeen outfit.

Rougvie arrived at the Dons via Dunfermline United's under-16 team, where he had

Billy Mc Neill's contribution to the Gothenburg success should not be underplayed

won the Scottish Juvenile Cup. He had initially been a target for Leeds United but when the Elland Road club decided their youth ranks had no vacancies, the Yorkshire side's scout Andy Young recommended the strapping teenager to his friend Jimmy Bonthrone at Pittodrie.

As a 16 year-old he was farmed out to Aberdeen junior side Rosemount by the Pittodrie club and the following term he was sent to the Highland League to step up a grade with Keith in 1973. He won the Highland League Cup with the Aberdeenshire side before being recalled by his club. George Christie, who managed Rougvie at Keith, said at the time: "Doug is being retained by Aberdeen for next season and they want to see how he is shaping. The lad has shown a lot of improvement in his season with us and I think he'll make the grade as a centre half in the First Division. He has all the attributes."

Rougvie spent two years learning his trade in the second string before Falkirk came close with a bid to land him on loan in the 1976/77 season. Ally MacLeod, in charge of the Dons, said:" Rougvie figures in my future plans but I was willing to loan him to Falkirk to give him regular experience in the First Division knowing that I would have him back at the end of the season."

The switch to Brockville broke down when the Bairns refused to allow the player to continue to train with the Dons during his loan stint and Rougvie went on to establish himself in the Dons team as a defensive mainstay, although not in the central role most had predicted for the towering youngster.

If the influential trio were Bonthrone's legacy, Billy McNeill's contribution to the Gothenburg success should not be underplayed. It was McNeill who recruited Gordon Strachan, the fourth piece of the 1983 jigsaw to fall into place, in 1977 from Dundee.

He is the first of the Gothenburg heroes to have cost the club a fee, with McNeill parting with £40,000 and Jim Shirra in a cash plus player deal when Strachan switched from Dundee. The Edinburgh-born midfielder was the club captain at Dens Park but still only 20 and an under-21 international when the Dons snapped him up. From the day he made his his debut in a 1-0 win at Dundee United on November 5, 1977, he was an unmovable part of the Aberdeen team.

with the young prospect's weekly wage rising from £15 to £70 following his move to Pittodrie

Strachan made his move on November 3 1977 and McNeill said: "This may not be the biggest signing Aberdeen have ever made but, in my opinion, it could well become the best. Gordon is only 20 years old and the club can expect at least another 10 years from him.
"It's a great signing for the future and I'm sure the Pittodrie fans will come to realise his great ability. I have seen him on many occasions and he has seldom failed to impress me."

Strachan said: "In some ways I must admit to being sorry to leave Dens Park after six seasons but I must also say that the move to one of the country's top clubs really excites me."

The move also increased his spending power, with the young prospect's weekly wage rising from £15 to £70 following his move to Pittodrie.

It was also McNeill who first tried the Miller-McLeish partnership, the pairing which became so vital to Ferguson during the run to Gothenburg. McNeill's hand was forced when he handed McLeish his debut in the New Year win against Dundee United in 1978, with the rookie drafted in after Willie Garner had broken curfew and been dropped. McLeish was a 17 year-old when he was thrown in at the deep end by McNeill but under Ferguson's tutelage he grew in stature, gained experience and went on to become a Scotland mainstay.

McLeish joined from juvenile side Glasgow United. He said: "Dumbarton, Hibs and a couple of English clubs were interested in me but Aberdeen were the first to ask me to sign, so I jumped at the chance. I played at right back for my school team and Hibs were interested in me in that position – but I prefer playing as a sweeper and being able to read the game from the middle of the defence." Even as a 17 year-old, the tall defender talked a good game.

Manager Ally MacLeod compared the young recruit to Dons skipper Willie Young when he arrived in July 1976. He spent his first season on the Pittodrie books learning his trade with junior outfit Lewis United. He was appointed captain by Lewis in his final game as a gesture of their appreciation and manager Stuart McAra was one of many who predicted a bright future.

McAra, as he waved goodbye to McLeish in February 1977, said: "He has been a great success at New Advocates Park and we are very disappointed to see him go. It means changing the most successful defence in the league – but we wish him all the best for the future. I have no doubt that he will make the grade at senior level because he is a very talented youngster. He has been one of the main reasons for our great run this season."

McLeish proved him right with a rapid rise to prominence at club and international level.

Jim Leighton was the first player thrown into the mix by Alex Ferguson. When the new manager arrived in the summer of 1978 he turned to the 20 year-old Johnstone-born goalkeeper to take over from veteran Bobby Clark and was not let down. Leighton went on to become the finest keeper of his generation, a Scotland legend and World Cup veteran. He had to be patient, deputising for Clark on and off until finally being handed the gloves permanently in 1980.

Leighton attended trials at Aberdeen alongside Alex McLeish, John McMaster and fellow goalkeeper John Gardiner having been spotted by scout John McNab. St Mirren, then led by Alex Ferguson were also keen on Leighton, as were Morton, but the lure of a full-time contract at Pittodrie swayed him.

Leighton, who signed during the Ally MacLeod era, was allowed to continue his development on the west coast with junior side Dalry Thistle, who were managed by Danish goalkeeper Eric Sorensen.

Billy McNeill chose to farm his promising young shot stopper out to Highland League side Deveronvale, with John Gardiner and Ally MacLean also on the books and vying for a place in the reserve team as understudies to Bobby Clark.

Leighton would train at Pittodrie in the morning, work in an Aberdeen sports shop in the afternoon and turn out for Vale every weekend. He was named as the Banff club's player of the year in 1978 before earning his big break in the Dons first team after Clark had suffered a hand injury.

Mark McGhee arrived seven months after Leighton had made his debut and marked a considerable investment by Ferguson as he began to put his distinctive mark on the Pittodrie squad. McGhee cost £80,000 when he joined from Newcastle in March 1979 at the age of 21, the former Morton youngster not realising he would go on to become the leading scorer in his new side's most memorable European adventure and justify his price tag several times over.

McGhee was Ferguson's first big money buy, but it was a bargain. The 21 year-old player, who had shot to prominence as leading scorer with Morton with a haul of 60 goals in just two seasons, had cost the English side £150,000 just 15 months earlier but was allowed to return to Scotland after failing to hold down a first team place.

After his first training session with his new team-mates, McGhee said: "I don't expect to walk right into the side. It is going to be a hard fight and it is up to me to play my way in. I'm happy to be an Aberdeen player. I've always regarded Aberdeen as the team most likely to break the Old Firm's stranglehold on Scottish football and I'm hoping I can do my bit in taking honours to Pittodrie."

He had been out of the Newcastle team for two months when Ferguson made his move but the wily Dons manager had seen enough of his target during his prolific Morton days to know he could cut it in the Premier Division.

Eight months after McGhee arrived in the north-east, a local youngster was blooded by Ferguson. The 16 year-old former Middlefield Boys Club player wearing the No.11 shirt in the 2-0 win against St Mirren on a December afternoon in 1979 went by the name of John Hewitt. That was the first time the name had been noted, but far from the last. Hewitt was gradually blended into the Dons side under Ferguson but by 1981 he was cemented in the starting 11 and went on to win medal after medal before his crowning moment in Gothenburg.

It took Alex Ferguson two attempts to land Hewitt, who was hot property as a schoolboy at Hilton Academy in Aberdeen. Ferguson tried to tempt the player to St Mirren when he was in charge at Love Street at a time when Celtic, Manchester United, Sheffield United and Middlesbrough were scouting him.

When he took over at Pittodrie, Ferguson returned to his old target and snapped up the eager 15 year-old Middlefield Boys Club starlet in the summer of 1978 on an S-form. The Dons boss said: "He's a natural goalscorer and those are in very short supply. If the boy is prepared to work he could have a great future."

Hewitt had been a ball boy at Pittodrie as a youngster and the schoolboy international's first choice was always to join his home town team.

Another home grown talent was next to burst onto the scene as the blocks fell into place. Neale Cooper, born in India but raised in Aberdeen and a product of the King Street Boys Club, was given his first start in October 1980 in a 2-0 win against Kilmarnock. The 16 year-old had also been a ball boy at Pittodrie just a few years earlier but Ferguson admired his determination and tenacity and viewed him as a key man for the future. He was proved right during the Euro run.

he went on to skipper Scotland's youth squad and made his debut at the age of 16 for the Dons

Cooper was signed on schoolboy forms for Aberdeen after catching the eye with his performance for King Street in the juvenile leagues and with Hazlehead Academy. As a 15 year-old, training with Scotland's youth team, he was singled out by coach Andy Roxburgh for his enthusiasm and ability and benefited from sessions under Walter Smith and Craig Brown amongst others during SFA gatherings at Largs.

He went on to skipper Scotland's professional youth squad and made his debut at the age of 16 for the Dons against Kilmarnock at Pittodrie.

Ferguson had no qualms about blooding him at such a tender age and said: "Despite his youth, Neale is above reserve team football standards and with the other Aberdeen defenders playing so well at the moment, this could be the best time to promote him so that he does not suffer from lack of support as he adjusts to Premier Division football."

Cooper headed into the 1981/82 season, his first as a senior pro, with his appetite whetted. He said: "There's something special about Premier Division matches. The atmosphere is good and I would like to get involved in more in the new season, but I'll just have to take it as it comes. With Willie Miller and Alex McLeish in the centre of defence, it makes it difficult to win a first team place in my usual position – to say the least."

Cooper had to be versatile to force his way into the Dons team and his ability to slot effortlessly into a variety of positions made him vital to the squad.

Two months later another of Fergie's young guns was fired on the road to stardom. Neil Simpson, born in London but brought up in Newmachar, had emerged at Middlefield Boys Club and was already a Scotland under-17 and under-18 international under Andy Roxburgh by the time he made his club debut in December 1980 in a 1-1 draw at Partick Thistle. He did enough in that appearance to convince Ferguson he had unearthed another gem and Simpson, despite his tender years, played out the remainder of the campaign as a first choice pick.

Simpson began his football journey in inauspicious surroundings, turning out for the local cub pack's side as well as his school team. He went on to star for Middlefield in the Aberdeen juvenile leagues.

He caught the eye of a string of clubs as a teenager and had trials with Manchester City, Aston Villa, Sheffield United and Middlesborough. Like so many, he opted against the bright lights of England to stay closer to home and signed for the Dons as a 15 year-old on schoolboy forms before stepping up to the full-time staff the following year.

Scotland youth coach Andy Roxburgh was soon alerted to his potential and Simpson became a key part of the national under-18 team before moving on to gain under-21 honours and being capped at senior level.

John Hewitt had made the No.10 shirt his own

The new look Aberdeen squad was taking shape as the preparations for the 1981/82 season began. Leighton was established as a quality goalkeeper, the Miller and McLeish partnership was rock solid and well supported by Rougvie. In midfield there were good options with Strachan on the right wing, Simpson through the middle and Neale Cooper able to slot in either in defence or further forward. McGhee was a potent threat and John Hewitt had made the No.10 shirt his own. The key ingredients were in place but Ferguson was not finished, he wanted the icing on the cake.

Peter Weir was recruited from St Mirren in the summer of 1981 after a lengthy pursuit. He was 23 by the time he moved north from St Mirren but had been a long time target for the Dons manager, who helped launch the left winger's career while he was still in charge of the Buddies. Weir was already an international and was an expensive acquisition, costing £200,000 and Ian Scanlon in part-exchange.

Weir was by far the most financially significant signing in the Gothenburg team. The deal was worth at £330,000 when the value of part-exchange was taken into account.

It made Weir the most expensive player in the history of the Scottish league but he took it in his stride. The winger said: "I feel I am joining the best club in Scotland. This will be an opportunity to further my ambitions – hopefully both at club level and international level. I know I'll be in good company and want quickly to become part of the team. I'm just glad the club saw fit to buy me."

Ferguson's pursuit of his former St Mirren protégé had lasted more than a year before the Buddies finally conceded the switch was inevitable. The Pittodrie manager said: "I am delighted to secure this player. All last season he was unavailable and even now I think Saints would have preferred him to go south."

St Mirren were accused of under-pricing Weir in some sections of the media, with figures of £500,000 deemed realistic, but the Love Street club was not in a position to turn down what was still an attractive offer from Aberdeen and the deal was done. Weir started the season in the Dons team and was joined three months later by an upcoming striker called Eric Black. Born in Bellshill, Black had been spotted further north playing school football in the Highlands as a pupil at Alness. His eye for goal and aerial ability made him stand out and at the age of 18 he was sent out to prove his first team worth by Ferguson, scoring in a 1-1 draw at home to Dundee United.

Black, whose father had starred for Airdrie and Hearts, was picked up early by Aberdeen and made the journey from his Highland home in Invergordon to train regularly with the Dons from the age of 13 while playing for Alness Academy. A touch of fortune surrounded the find, with Alness teacher Ian Mackenzie writing to the Dons to suggest they take an interest in the youngster who was leading the line for his school team.

Youth coach Lenny Taylor followed up the interest and the relationship built from there, with Black signing as an S-form before becoming a professional at the age of 16. He had also trained with Highland League outfit Ross County but his first visit to Pittodrie convinced him that Aberdeen were the club for him. Billy McNeill was in charge when the initial invitation to train with the Dons was sent out but Alex Ferguson was the gaffer by the time the arrangements were put in place.

FIRST ROUND: ABERDEEN v DINAMO TIRANA
SEPTEMBER 15, 1982: ABERDEEN 1, DINAMO TIRANA 0   SEPTEMBER 29, 1982: DINAMO TIRANA 0, ABERDEEN 0

A **"perilous"** trip to face "stuffy" opposition. That was the summary of the first round tie against Dinamo Tirana of Albania before Aberdeen had even kicked a ball in the 1982/83 European campaign.

The Dons knew exactly what their prize would be if they could overcome Sion in the preliminary stage, with the first round draw already made and Tirana awaiting the winners of the Scotland v Switzerland contest.

The men from Pittodrie became only the fourth Scottish side to venture to Albania, with former manager Billy McNeill providing a useful dossier having taken Celtic to play Partizan Tirana just three seasons before.

There were several hurdles to overcome, with red tape among them. For Celtic's trip in the European Cup the authorities in the eastern European country refused to grant visas for the press following the Parkhead side.

In Aberdeen's case, even the playing staff had to wait until just days before the party flew out to discover if they would receive clearance from the Albanians to enter the country. In the end they were granted visas for 22 players, leaving Ferguson with a decision to make on who to take with him, while six sportswriters were also permitted to travel. It was the largest media contingent ever allowed into Albania but Ian Taggart, Aberdeen's secretary, was not so lucky and had his application for a visa denied. The club chartered an Aer Lingus plane, with the Irish firm one of the few airlines permitted to land on Albanian soil.

Dinamo were a part-time side of amateur players but that status belied their ability, having won their national cup 13 times and crowned league champions on 14 occasions prior to the match against Aberdeen.

They played the first leg at Pittodrie and set out to frustrate, indulging in time wasting and doing their best to kill the pace of the game. The return leg was switched from Dinamo's home ground, which had a capacity of 15,000 at the time, to the larger national Qermal Stafa Stadium.

The Dons were unfamiliar with the surroundings but well prepared for the conditions they would face, packing plentiful supplies of salt tablets to combat the draining heat which raced into the 90s. After taking advice from officials at Irish club Linfield, who had been at the same stadium on European Cup duty the previous week, Alex Ferguson also opted to ship hampers of food to Albania. The inventory included corned beef, fruit salad, corn flakes, long-life milk, lemonade, and bottles of water for the two day stay.

Ferguson, speaking before the second leg on foreign soil, said: "There is no denying that the heat could cause us a bit of a problem – but Linfield had more complaints about the humidity. Linfield are a part-time club and maybe they had more difficulty in coping with conditions. Anyway, players such as Willie Miller, Alex McLeish and Gordon Strachan all played for Scotland during the World Cup in Spain in similar conditions."

In truth, nothing could have prepared them for what was in store. Aberdeen's flight touched down as news of an attempted coup in Albania broke. It was impossible to

● Mark McGhee shoots just over during Aberdeen's home encounter with Dinamo Tirana

make telephone calls in or out of the country, with Press and Journal writer Alastair MacDonald unable to report back after landing due to the troubles in the country but communications were restored prior to the tie. The coup attempt, the weekend before Aberdeen's trip, was thwarted when Albanian security forces shot dead a heavily armed group who they believed were preparing to launch a bid to overthrow the government.

Those dramatic developments did not detract from Aberdeen's Albanian experience. After touching back down at Aberdeen airport, where the return flight had been diverted from its scheduled destination of Edinburgh after an agreement was struck to keep the Granite city's airport open for a few minutes past its 9.30pm curfew, Ferguson reflected: "It was a great trip, one of our best in Europe. The hospitality was magnificent. The Albanians couldn't do enough for us."

The Dons were greeted on that September evening by a group of young fans who surely could not have guessed where the European adventure would end. Another tricky hurdle had been overcome but the Dons were made to work all the way to book their place in the second round by the narrowest of margins.

Albanian keeper's one error brings winner

DISAPPOINTING DONS

● *By Alastair Macdonald*

ABERDEEN	1
DINAMO TIRANA	0

● The Albanian keeper saves at the feet of Strachan and McGhee

ABERDEEN dispelled the mystery surrounding European Cup Winners' Cup first round opponents Dinamo Tirana at Pittodrie last night and revealed the Albanian side as only a moderate combine – but the Dons failed to take advantage of the absolute outfield superiority they enjoyed for the full 90 minutes.

The one goal advantage which Aberdeen take to Albania for the second leg in a fortnight was due to a blunder by Tirana goalkeeper Luarasi when he failed to hold a Doug Bell shot in the 29th minute and John Hewitt netted the rebound.

For the rest of the game the Albanian goal wore a charmed existence, Aberdeen's failure to score being due to a combination of abominable luck and their own finishing shortcomings.

As an indication of the Dons territorial supremacy, they had 10 corners to Tirana's one of the first half and the second half tally was 6-1 in Aberdeen's favour.

It was a night of frustration, both for the Aberdeen side and for the 15,100 spectators. The Albanian side don't strike me as being able to play much better, but going abroad with only a single goal margin will put the Dons under considerable strain in the second leg.

Tirana were not given much opportunity to attack but when they did break away Zeri looked the only attacker capable of worrying the Aberdeen defence.

The Dons employed both substitutes in the second half, with Neale Cooper and Eric Black replacing Doug Bell and Stuart Kennedy, but these changes and a consequent reshuffle of the Aberdeen line-up failed to change the pattern of play significantly.

ABERDEEN fulfilled their promise to attack from the kick-off but a first minute misunderstanding between Simpson and Miller almost on the half line allowed Dinamo to make an early break.

Zeri raced away with the ball but he elected to shoot from 25 yards and his try was wide of target.

News of the interpretation of the four step rule apparently had not filtered through to Albania for Luarasi was picked up for contravening it in the fourth minute with Aberdeen being awarded an indirect free kick inside the penalty box. Simpson back heeled the free to Strachan whose shot was blocked on line.

A minute later Ruci was booked for tripping Weir after the Aberdeen winger had rounded him.

The Dons piled on the pressure an McGhee had a shot cleared almo involuntarily from the line by Kug

There was another goal-li clearance in the eighth minute wh Targai kicked clear with Weir close attendance.

With the Albanian defence und

John Hewitt slots homes the only goal of the game

...ere pressure a McGhee cut back ...ed to find a team-mate, and the ...d was eventually scrambled clear.

...0 yard drive by Simpson in 14 ...nutes was punched away, double ...ed, by Luarasi and the Albanian ...per was again lucky to be in direct ...e to save a Simpson shot a minute ...er following a goalmouth ...amble.

...inking run by Bell in 21 minutes ...ught the Dons a corner but ...Ghee's header from Weir's flag ...k went straight to the keeper.

...e Albanian defenders were ...nceding free kicks with gay ...andon and from one of these ...tside the penalty box McMaster ...d a try deflected for a corner.

...arasi, under constant siege, again ...ed a double fisted punch to save a ...ll flick from a McMaster cross.

...ighton had his first direct save in ...minutes but he was untroubled by ...Kanai shot.

...erdeen broke the deadlock in the ...minutes when HEWITT scored ...er a Bell shot had bounced off the ...eper's chest.

...namo won their first corner three ...inutes later but it only led to a free

kick for Aberdeen.

Gega was the next Albanian to fall foul of the referee when he was shown the yellow card for a foul on Strachan in 42 minutes, and just on the interval Kanai was booked after tripping Weir.

The Tirana goal had a narrow escape when a Rougvie header rebounded from the goalkeeper's foot and Hewitt's try from the rebound was also blocked on the line.

Aberdeen started the second half where they left off before the interval – on the attack.

Luarasi again showed his preference for punching clearances when he fisted away a Hewitt header from a Weir cross.

The Albanian keeper did well to block a close range try by Hewitt with his body in 52 minutes, and McMaster's 25 yard try from the rebound rattled the crossbar.

Rougvie was frequently up with his forwards in the Tirana penalty box and he was twice just wide of target with headers.

In 57 minutes Aberdeen substituted Neale Cooper for Doug Bell and

continued their assault on the Dinamo goal.

The Belgian referee ignored a penalty claim in 63 minutes when Xhafa seemed to arm the ball in the penalty box.

Two minutes later Luarasi finger tipped a 25 yard shot from Simpson over the crossbar and then Miller joined in the act, but his header from a Weir cross was also too high.

Aberdeen made a second substitution in 68 minutes with Eric Black replacing Stuart Kennedy. Rougvie moved to right back with Cooper taking over in the middle of defence.

The newcomer was soon in the action but his first header was off target.

The Tirana goal luck continued when Black sent a header wide of the target from a Strachan cross in 80 minutes and three minutes later McGhee had the miss of the game, hooking the ball over the bar from inside the six yard box.

Zeri, Tirana's only dangerous raider, was not far off target with a try in 84 minutes when the ball rebounded to him following a free kick.

With two minutes to go McGhee had the ball in the net from a Strachan pass but the referee indicated offside.

ABERDEEN – Leighton, Kennedy (Black), McMaster, Bell (Cooper), Rougvie, Miller, Strachan, Simpson, McGhee, Hewitt, Weir.

DINAMO TIRANA – Luarasi, Kugi, Bragu, Targai, Ruci, Xhafa (Dauti), Gega (Musai), Janai, Zeri, Fagekugi, Demorraii.

Referee – L. Deisemme (Belgium).

Great night for Scotland as Aberdeen, Celtic, Dundee United and Rangers march on in Europe

CUP JOY FOR SUPER DONS

DINAMO TIRANA	0
ABERDEEN	0

(Aggregate 0-1)

● *By Alastair Macdonald*

A WORKMANLIKE display of controlled, disciplined football in sauna like conditions saw Aberdeen safely through to the second round of the European Cup Winners' Cup in the Albanian capital yesterday afternoon.

Despite the urging of a near capacity 20,000 crowd in the Qemai Stafa Stadium, Dinamo failed to make the slightest impression on the one-goal lead the Dons held from the first leg at Pittodrie as Aberdeen took the honours in every aspect of the game.

It was an unspectacular 90 minutes, but the real merit of the Aberdeen performance lay in the efficiency with which they played a style of football completely foreign to their natural instincts – a style which, nevertheless, is a necessary attribute for any side with European aspirations.

Attempting – in the event, successfully – to combat the enervating heat and humidity by an economy of movement, the Dons still contrived to pose a greater threat to the Tirana goal than the Albanians did to the Aberdeen goal.

Dinamo, showing three changes from the fist leg, looked no more impressive than they did at Pittodrie, and their finishing was particularly ineffectual on the few occasions they were given a glimpse of the Aberdeen goal. With only a single-goal cushion, however, the Dons could never discount the possibility of the Albanians scoring a fluke goal.

The Aberdeen players, howeve kept their composu throughout, not least in th restraint they showed in the fa of physical provocation fro their Tirana counterparts.

In the final minute of the gam the referee eventually book Gega, the Dinamo defender w suffered a similar fate in the fir leg, but up to that point t Hungarian official steadfas pursued a safe middle course his decisions, even to the extent turning down penalty clai from both sides.

The entire Aberdeen tea including second-half substitu John McMaster and Jo Hewitt, contributed to a fir class performance, but worthy special mention were Wi Miller for his inspiratio leadership and example, a Doug Bell and Neil Simpson their Trojan efforts in midfiel

A momentary lapse in

berdeen defence gave Dinamo eir first scoring chance in the 12 inutes but a Demorraii shot was ide of target.

few minutes later Bell reatened the Dinamo goal in a reakthrough.

elia was the next Albanian ayer to have a go at the berdeen goal, but his long range fort went over the bar and there emed a better chance of a goal the other end in 24 minutes hen a Bell cross from the left as met by McGhee, who could ot control the ball.

he Dons' best scoring chance me in 27 minutes when a eir cross was headed own by McGhee, but uarasi blocked impson's shot with his et.

eighton came to the ons' rescue in 32 minutes ith a diving save to his left to rn a shot from Kanai round the ost.

eri sent a shot over the crossbar 36 minutes but, as the lbanians became more rustrated, the Dons started to unch their own attacks and in 9 minutes Weir struck the rossbar with a fierce shot after trachan had touched on a ennedy cross.

berdeen claimed what seemed be a reasonable penalty in 42 inutes when Weir was grounded y Dauti, but the Hungarian

referee waved away the Dons' claims.

A minute after the resumption Kanai made a break from his own penalty area but a fine piece of acceleration by Bell enabled the Aberdeen midfield player to rob him.

Two minutes later a long-range effort from Gega was safely held by Leighton.

Dinamo were unsuccessful with a penalty claim in 51 minutes when a Zeri shot seemed to strike Miller on his hand but the referee ignored the Albanian claims.

Dinamo made a substitution in 61 minutes when Noea replaced Dauti and a minute later Aberdeen brought on McMaster for Cooper.

The newcomer's first pass almost produced a goal. It allowed McGhee to race away but after beating one defender the Aberdeen striker was dispossessed by Gega at the expense of a corner.

Aberdeen might again have been awarded a penalty in 67 minutes when Bell was brought down by Targai but once more the referee turned a deaf ear.

Dinamo made their second substitution in 73 minutes, Agalliu replacing Demorraii, but it was Aberdeen who were dictating the play.

Bell made a promising break away in 77 minutes but he was finally obstructed by two defenders.

With five minute to go a Strachan-Miller-Kennedy counter attack on the right ended with the full back sending the ball over the bar and a minute later a magnificent 50-yard run by Simpson saw Luarasi made a fine save.

Aberdeen immediately substituted Hewitt for McGhee and continued to pressurise the Dinamo goal.

In 89 minutes Gega was booked for a foul on Strachan but the whistle brought and end to the magnificent effort by the Dons.

DINAMO TIRANA – Luarasi, Kugi, Dauti (Noea), Targai, Gega, Ruci, Delia, Kanai, Zeri, Marko, Demorraii (Agalliu).

ABERDEEN – Leighton, Kennedy, Rougvie, Cooper (McMaster), McLeish, Miller, Strachan, Simpson, McGhee (Hewitt), Bell, Weir.

Referee – J. Szaavo, Hungary.

THE SUPPORT CAST

CAN you can name the five men who played in Aberdeen's run to the European Cup Winners' Cup final but missed out on the chance to play their part in the glory of Gothenburg?

That unlucky group can rightly lay claim to a part in the most glittering occasion in the history of the club, some had key roles while others were more walk-on extras in the extraordinary story of the 1982/83 season.

The first and most significant absentee from the team to face Real Madrid is the only man from that famous Dons squad to have played alongside Alex Ferguson as well as for him: Stuart Kennedy. The defender was a team-mate of Ferguson as a youngster making his way in the game at Falkirk while his future gaffer wound down his own playing career.

The second on the list of misfortune is one of the few Dons players to have gone on to have crossed the great divide and played for arch rivals Rangers. He is Dougie Bell.

Coming in at number three is the member of the Gothenburg crop who has gone on to coach Motherwell, Hibs, Rangers, Scotland and Birmingham City. Andy Watson, the trusty sidekick of Alex McLeish, could play the game as well as teach it.

Fourth on the role of agony is a home-grown product, a Scotland schoolboy international from Northfield Academy who made his debut in continental competition in 1983. Willie Falconer helped the Dons through the semi-final against Waterschei but played no part in Gothenburg.

The other semi-final participant who had to watch from the sidelines as the drama unfolded in Sweden was Ian Angus, completing the list of players on the credits for the supporting cast.

It was an eclectic group but each was a piece in the jigsaw of that momentous season. For some it was the start of a football journey, for others close to the end, but behind every name is an intriguing story.

Kennedy's tale of woe is the most well worn yet remains the most emotive, one of the cruel twists in the happy tale. He was 20 days away from his 30th birthday when the Dons ran out at the Ullevi to tackle the mighty Real, it should have been an amazing period in his life but it turned into the darkest.

Kennedy was included on the bench for the final but he and his manager knew he was not fit enough to play a part as he battled against a knee injury. Ferguson is not known as the sentimental type but he showed his human side when he desperately tried to keep his wounded soldier involved.

It was Ferguson who had asked the defender to play through the pain in the semi-final against Waterschei despite toiling after suffering knee damage in the earlier Scottish Cup semi-final against Celtic. He played on manfully against the Belgians but when he twisted the same knee in the semi-final second leg it signalled his final contribution to a campaign which he had been such an integral part of.

he was the perfect modern defender, a right-back blessed with unbeatable pace and razor sharp timing

Confined to the dug-out for the Gothenburg game, he caught his studs in the gap between the track and pitch as he leapt to celebrate John Hewitt's winner and the further damage that caused to his already painful joint was the death knell for his career. Football life ended at the age of 30, when doctors confirmed his attempts at a comeback were in vain and advised him to turn his back on the profession he had lived and breathed since first dreaming of making it in the game. Kennedy would undoubtedly have played on well into the 1980s. He was the perfect modern defender, a right-back blessed with unbeatable pace and razor sharp timing. He was only booked twice in a distinguished top flight career, which included eight caps for Scotland, and he was proud of his disciplinary record and ability to play hard but fair.

The defender was an apprentice electrician when he teamed up with Alex Ferguson on the Falkirk playing staff in the early 1970s. He made his Bairns debut as an 18 year-old in 1971 and was snapped up by Aberdeen manager Ally MacLeod in 1976 to start a rollercoaster ride of highs and lows in the north-east and beyond.

He went on to win the League Cup in his first few months at Pittodrie as well as the Premier Division in 1980 and Scottish Cup in 1982. He also featured in the 1978 World Cup finals in Argentina.

Kennedy, who made 335 appearances for Aberdeen, was retained by his manager after the agony of his retirement but roles as a coach and scout did not fill him with optimism about his future in the game. For a man who was so influential in Aberdeen's greatest ever team it must have been painful to suddenly find himself looking in from the outside of the dressing room which had been his home.

Instead he quickly made the decision for a clean break from football and entered the licensed trade in Falkirk before selling his pub interests to concentrate on a bed and breakfast venture in Grangemouth.

Kennedy prefers to stay out of the limelight but in rare newspaper interviews the emotional end to his Dons days is never far from the surface. Speaking at the time of the club's centenary celebrations, he admitted: "I wasn't right, but managed to do enough to make the bench. As the final became more and more tense, the opportunity for Fergie to get me on to the field became less and less. I was absolutely gutted. Then when John Hewitt scored the winner to make it 2-1 I jumped on to the track, caught my studs between the track and the grass and twisted the knee again. I knew then it was bad and that was really the end.

Kennedy had not missed a single European tie prior to sitting out the final

"Dougie Bell, who destroyed Waterschei, also missed the final through injury and we talked about a suicide pact as everyone else celebrated. We joined in as much as we could, but it wasn't the same. It should have been the greatest night of our lives, but we felt awful."

"As I tried to recover from the injury I dreamed I would be all right and the big man up there would look after me, but it never happened. You have to cling on to something. I was doing a bit of scouting for Fergie and working with the reserves, but I felt I needed to get away from Pittodrie. It was great that the fans felt sympathy for me, but I couldn't handle it. It was too much to take and I decided to go back to my hometown of Grangemouth."

Kennedy had not missed a single European tie prior to sitting out the final, starting nine of the 10 games he featured in and making an appearance from the bench in the first leg of the second round tie against Lech Poznan.

Dougie Bell was not far behind Kennedy on the European Cup Winners' Cup appearance list for the season, making eight starts from a possible 11, and was a creative force in the team of 1983.

Injury robbed Bell of a place in the team for the final and he also sat out the 3-2 victory against Bayern Munich as well as the 1-0 defeat against Waterschei in the second leg of the semi-final. Other than that, he was in the thick of the continental action. He starred against Bayern Munich in Germany and was man of the match in the 5-1 semi-final first leg trouncing of Wateschei.

Crucially the Paisley born star had been on the scoresheet against Lech Poznan in the second leg of the second round, grabbing the only goal of the game to clinch a 3-0 aggregate win.

A knee ligament injury in the Scottish Cup semi-final win against Celtic, the same match which caused Kennedy so much pain and anguish, was responsible for his stuttering finish to a season which promised so much.

Just as the manager had attempted to keep Kennedy's spirits up by keeping him involved at Pittodrie, Bell's heartbreak was tempered slightly by the award of a new three year contract within weeks of the Gothenburg triumph.

It was little surprise that Alex Ferguson wanted to keep hold of the player.

Brought up in Cumbernauld, Bell moved into the senior ranks when Ferguson spotted his potential and recruited him for St Mirren as a 19 year-old. When Bell was freed by the Buddies in 1979 it was Ferguson who again took a chance on the midfielder, this time signing him for the Dons.

Bell did not see out the 36 month deal he penned in the summer of 1983. The arrival of the silky skilled Jim Bett two years later signalled the end of his first team days with the Dons and his transfer request was granted.

Chelsea and St Mirren were immediately on his tail but the six figure valuation placed on the midfielder's head by Ferguson and the Pittodrie board cooled their interest.

That opened the door for Rangers, under Jock Wallace, to begin haggling and eventually a £120,000 fee was agreed for the Scotland under-21 international.

Bell, a childhood fan of the Ibrox club, returned to the west coast but the road was not paved with gold.

His stint in Light Blue lasted just 16 months as he found himself surplus to requirements as new manager Graeme Souness began his big money revolution.

Hibs provided an escape route at the start of 1987 and Bell developed a wanderlust.

He went on to turn out for Shrewsbury, Hull, Birmingham City, Portadown, Partick Thistle, Clyde, Elgin City, Alloa and Albion Rovers. He is now part of the coaching staff at Clyde.

Andy Watson's contribution to the run was limited to two appearances. He came on from the bench in the 1-0 win against Lech Poznan in the second leg of the second round and was in the starting line-up, wearing the No.10 shirt, for the semi-final second leg which ended in a 1-0 defeat against Waterschei.

In recent years Watson's profile has risen in tandem with Alex McLeish and his progress up the managerial ladder to international level and more recently the English top flight.

he was the only Aberdeen-born player in the 1980 Premier Division side and by the tender age of 22 had 100 appearances

Watson has been there every step of the way with McLeish on that journey but there is more to the man than a coaching pedigree. The Aberdonian made 135 starts and a further 42 substitute's appearances for his home town club between 1977 and 1983. A total of 26 of those games were in the 1982/83 campaign but he had to be content to act as a squad man in Gothenburg.

As a promising youngster at Hilton Academy a career with the Dons was the obvious route but in fact it was Middlesbrough who made the first move in the face of competition from Queens Park Rangers, Sunderland and Aston Villa.

Jack Charlton at Boro thought he had clinched the hard working and skilful midfielder but Aberdeen stepped in early in 1976 to trump the English admirers.

He cut his teeth with Sunnyside in the juvenile ranks and Rosemount in the juniors, picking up Scotland caps at schoolboy and youth level, before stepping up to the Dons first team.

He was the only Aberdeen-born player in the 1980 Premier Division winning side and by the tender age of 22 had 100 appearances under his belt and had four Scotland under-21 games to his credit.

As the dominant team of the 1980s began to take shape he began to find himself relegated to the fringes but the manager still wanted him at Pittodrie, rejecting a £50,000 bid from Leeds United in the months leading up to the European final.

The Elland Road side were not deterred and within weeks of the European Cup Winners' Cup landing on the Pittodrie sideboard they signed the midfielder for £60,000.

At the tail end of 1984 Watson returned to Scotland with Hearts and in 1986 crossed the capital to sign for Hibs before retiring from football in 1989, at the age of 29, due to a knee injury.

At the time Watson said: "It has been a traumatic time but hopefully things will work out."

He could never have predicted just how much of an understatement that was. Things turned out better than okay. He won a full-time coaching role at Easter Road after hanging up his boots before stepping up to become assistant manager to McLeish at Motherwell.

The duo went from Fir Park to Hibs to Rangers, despite Watson's childhood allegiances to Celtic. He tasted domestic success with the Ibrox side before savouring the highs of Scotland life during the amazing Euro 2008 qualification bid and then transferring their talents to the Premiership with Birmingham City late in 2007. The old adage that management can never be a substitute for playing appears, in Watson's case, to be false. As a player he had a steady but unspectacular time, as a coach he has catapulted himself among the elite at home and abroad.

Willie Falconer's cameo on the road to Gothenburg was a surreal one. He made his first appearance for Aberdeen on one of the biggest night's the club ever experienced – making his entrance in the second leg of the semi-final as the Dons celebrated their passage to their first ever European final.

The game ended in a 1-0 defeat away to Waterschei in Belgium but it did not matter, a 5-2 aggregate victory had been secured.

Falconer, a Northfield Academy pupil who had been capped by Scotland schoolboys, only made one other appearance in his rookie season but the boss had no qualms about giving him a taste of the big occasion. Match number two was a 1-0 home win in the league against Celtic.

The 17 year-old Mastrick boy, a product of Aberdeen Lads Club and Lewis United, got the shout he had been waiting for half way through the second period against Waterschei.

He admitted at the time: "If anyone said to me a week ago that I would be making my first team debut in Belgium I would have told them they were dreaming. I really thought I was there to make up the numbers. It was different from anything I had ever experienced before and it seemed to be over in no time. My debut almost had a dream ending because one cross I had from the wing almost beat the keeper – but maybe that was asking a bit too much."

Despite his encouraging start, the powerfully built striker had to be patient as he attempted to establish himself as an Aberdeen player. He did not become a regular until the 1987/88 season, when manager Ian Porterfield successfully converted him from a forward to a defender. At home on the left side of the back four and equally comfortable as a centre-half or sweeper, it was a change in direction the player was happy with. He started 32 league games that term, having been a bit-part man up to that stage, but the campaign turned sour when he was dropped for the Scottish Cup semi-final against Dundee United. The fact it was David Robertson who took his place, a player who was destined to leave Pittodrie for Rangers, was a bitter pill to swallow.

He knew then that his future was away from the north-east and a stream of English clubs were alerted. Norwich City, Leicester City, Bradford and Aston Villa all expressed an interest but Watford, with a £300,000 offer, were the club which got its man.

Falconer served with distinction in England during spells with Watford, Middlesbrough and Sheffield United before Celtic lured him north in 1994. He went on to play for Motherwell, Dundee, Clydebank, St Johnstone, Grimsby and Clyde before retiring in 2003.

Ian Angus also had a solitary European match against his record in 1982/83. He came on from the bench in the same game as Falconer but he already had a healthy dose of first team experience by that stage. The Glaswegian was 21 when he took his place in the Gothenburg squad and in his third season as a fully fledged first team man.

Angus made his Dons debut as a 19 year-old having been recruited from Eastercraigs Boys Club in his home city. While he had a fleeting role to play in the success of the 1982/83 season he went on to establish himself as a key performer in the 1984/85 campaign as the club swept to the Premier Division title. He had made 12 appearances in the league title success the previous term.

> *in the modern game it is incredible to comprehend a team progressing to the final of a European competition using a pool of just 17 players*

In the summer of 1986 he joined Dundee as part of the deal which took Robert Connor in the opposite direction and remained at Dens Park until a £40,000 transfer to Motherwell in 1990. Angus went on to net the third goal for Well in the 4-3 Scottish Cup final victory against Dundee United in 1991 to cap his first season in Lanarkshire in style. He crashed through the 100 appearance mark for the Steelmen over a four year period and went on to turn out for Clyde and Albion Rovers in the latter stages of his career.

In the modern game it is incredible to comprehend a team progressing to the final of a European competition using a pool of just 17 players but that was all it took for the well oiled machine of Aberdeen to roll forward. The strength was in the unit and those on the fringes new their role was purely to deputise for the men in possession, the manager knew his best team and he stuck with unless injury forced his hand. It was inevitable that there would be casualties along the way but there was a contingency for every occasion and the Dons had a reserve pool packed with enthusiasm, talent and passion. Every one of the 17 had a part to play in the manager's masterplan.

SECOND ROUND: ABERDEEN v LECH POZNAN
OCTOBER 20, 1982: ABERDEEN 2, LECH POZNAN 0   NOVEMBER 3, 1982: LECH POZNAN 0, ABERDEEN 1

ABERDEEN had never before made it through to the quarter-final of a European competition. Standing between them and that landmark in the second round was Polish side Lech Poznan.

Wins in both legs booked a berth in the last eight for the Dons, who joined an eclectic mix of teams in the draw. Real Madrid were by far the most feared name in the hat but Barcelona, Inter Milan, Bayern Munich and Paris St Germain, inspired by Argentina star Ossie Ardiles, had also made it through. The Dons were in a group of three rank outsiders, joined by Austria Vienna and Belgian outfit Waterschei.

Lech were dumped out of the competition by their Scottish opponents after two disciplined and professional performances from the Reds.

Going into the first leg at Pittodrie the Dons were deprived of Stuart Kennedy's presence in the back four. The influential full-back had missed three games with an ankle injury and, despite being passed fit to take his place in the squad, Kennedy was not considered ready to start and had to be content with a place on the bench.

Archie Knox had been sent to Poland to watch Lech in action and his reports led Alex Ferguson to boldly claim Aberdeen would need to establish at least a two goal cushion on home turf to have any chance of progressing. He backed up his words with actions, sacrificing the defensive strength of Doug Rougvie to accommodate Eric Black in an attacking line-up.

Aberdeen at least had form. The last time a Polish side had visited Pittodrie, Gornik Zabrze were defeated 5-0 in a friendly encounter in 1970.

The 100 per cent record was maintained in less spectacular fashion with the 2-0 first leg victory, a win which Ferguson declared himself "reasonably happy" with. The hard to please manager must surely have been ecstatic when the job was completed with a 1-0 win in Poznan.

The two triumphs came against a Lech side with six current or former Polish internationals in their ranks, although they entered the first leg on the back of two league defeats.

Poland, who had claimed the bronze medal at the 1982 World Cup, were a major force in European football but that did not daunt a Dons side growing in confidence with each passing tie.

40

DONS TO THE DOUBLE WITH POSITIVE RESULT

ABERDEEN	2
LECH POZNAN	0

● *By Alastair Macdonald*

ABERDEEN took a significant step towards achieving their goal of a place in the quarter-finals of the European Cup Winners' Cup when they seized a two goal advantage from the firt leg of their second round tie at Pittodrie last night.

Despite dominating the outfield from the kick-off, it looked for a long time as if Aberdeen's recent shortcomings in finishing would again prove their downfall as they hammered the Poznan goal in front of a 17,600 crowd.

Two goals in the space of as many minutes early in the second half, however, gave the Dons the cushion they were looking for to carry forward to the second leg in Poland in a fortnight.

Yet the Dons' lead could easily have been much more clear cut as on three occasions their scoring efforts were foiled by the woodwork.

Eric Black struck the crossbar twice and Gordon Strachan saw one of his tries rebound from upright.

The Poznan side, on last night's showing, do not appear to present an insurmountable hurdle for the Dons. The Poles' attacking was restricted to breakaway raids and at no time was goalkeeper Jim Leighton seriously tested.

Lech, however, did show bursts of pace in their build-up and they could be a different proposition on their own ground.

The Dutch referee gave an early indication of how he intended to handle the game when he awarded half a dozen free kicks in the opening 90 seconds. There was barely physical contact in some of the incidents.

Aberdeen won their first corner in two minutes. Weir's flag kick was met by McLeish whose shot was blocked and McGhee hooked the ball wide of the goal from the rebound.

A minute later Black headed wide from a McMaster cross.

Lech's first break in the eighth minute saw Okonski send a 20-yard shot over the crossbar.

A minute later play returned to the other end with Bell shooting wide from a layback from McGhee.

With play constantly interrupted by the referee's whistle, frequently for the most trifling of offences, there was little continuity.

Aberdeen were maintaining steady pressure on the Polish goal but Plesnierowicz showed great confidence in cutting out cross-balls anywhere near his six yards box.

The Lech keeper demonstrated that he was equally capable in dealing with direct shots when he held a 20-yard drive from Strachan in 19 minutes.

A McMaster try in the 23rd minute seemed to be on target but it was deflected by Adamiec for a corner.

A back head flick by Black from

Weir's flag kick was scrambled off the line by the keeper after he had failed to hold the ball at the first attempt.

Lech's attacks were confined to breakaways and in one of these by Strugarek in 27 minutes Miller made a decisive tackle from which the Aberdeen skipper took some time to recover.

Plesnierowicz came to Lech's rescue in 33 minutes with a fine save from a close-range header by Black from a Weir cross.

Five minutes before the interval a Pawlak cross was deflected to the feet of Okonski and his hurried shot went just outside Leighton's left-hand post.

A minute later McMaster sent a low shot just wide following a Strachan free kick.

The Dons came closest to scoring just on the interval when Weir nudged a McGhee cross past the Polish keeper but Black's header rebounded from the crossbar.

The second half opened with Cooper sending a speculative try over Lech's crossbar after an upfield foray.

Four minutes into the second period Strugarek was booked for a touch-line tackle on Black and a minute later Bell sent a try just over the bar.

It just wasn't Black's day and in the 51st minute he was foiled by the crossbar for the second time when he sent in a great 25-yard shot which had the Polish keeper beaten but the ball rebounded from the woodwork.

Plesnierowicz brought off another fine save, diving full length to hold a Bell header from a Weir cross in 54 minutes, but the Dons made the vital breakthrough a minute later when McGHEE found the net with a header from a Weir flag kick – Aberdeen's ninth corner of the game.

The Poznan side replied to the goal by bursting into Aberdeen territory and a cross from Bak went across the Aberdeen goalface.

Aberdeen, having tasted blood, struck again in 57 minutes when, after a fine run into the penalty box by Strachan, WEIR met his team-mate's cross and turned the ball past the Polish keeper.

Lech made a substitution in 60 minutes when Niewiadomski took over from Kupewicz, who had never looked completely fit,

Szewczyk had to go behind the goal for treatment in 65 minutes but he soon resumed.

Aberdeen made a substitution in 71 minutes when Kennedy replaced Bell. Cooper switched to left back with McMaster moving forward into midfield.

A second Polish substitution followed two minutes later when Krzyanowski replaced Strugarek.

A Strachan break into the penalty box from a Weir pass brought disappointment for the midfield player when his left-foot shot rebounded from the base of the left-hand upright.

A McGhee-Strachan move in 79 minutes ended with Strachan having his final shot charged down by the keeper and McGhee mis-hit the rebound wide of goal.

This was followed a minute later by Aberdeen's second substitution, with Hewitt coming on for Black.

The Lech goal had a narrow escape in 86 minutes when Hewitt just failed to connect with a Strachan grounder into the goalmouth.

ABERDEEN – Leighton, Cooper, McMaster, Bell (Kennedy), McLeish, Miller, Strachan, Simpson, McGhee, Black (Hewitt), Weir.

LECH POZNAN – Plesnierowicz, Pawlak, Snewczyk, Adamiec, Barczak, Strugarek (Krzyanowski), Kupewicz (Niewiadomski), Oblewski, Malek, Okonski, Bak.

Referee – E. Mulder (Holland).

POLISHED DONS MAKE EUROPEAN HISTORY

LECH POZNAN	0
ABERDEEN	1

(Aggregate 0-3)

● *By Alastair Macdonald reports from Poznan*

A LONG-STANDING barrier was broken down in Poznan's Bulgarska Stadium yesterday when a disciplined Aberdeen team wrote a new chapter of club history by booking a place in the quarter-final of a European tournament for the first time in 15 years of trying.

The second-leg victory which the Dons achieved on an outsize pitch to complete a 3-0 aggregate elimination of Polish Cup holders Lech Poznan was the product of a thoroughly professional, if not entirely brilliant, performance by the PIttodrie side which eventually earned the acclaim of a vociferous 30,000 Polish crowd.

A 59th minute goal, scored by Doug Bell, with considerable assistance from Peter Weir and Mark McGhee, signalled the death of Lech's last lingering hopes of salvaging this second-round tie, but the spadework of the Dons' triumph was done long before that.

Only in the early stages of a game played in near perfect weather conditions for football – dull, but mild – was there any real threat to Aberdeen's supremacy.

A nervous start with the midfield failing to take an early grip of the play subjected the Dons to pressure un-necessarily in the opening half-hour. Fortunately, however, the advantage they thus conceded to Poznan in this period was negated partly by the inaccurate finishing of the Polish side, but principally by the superb form of Aberdeen's back four.

Not only did the Dons' rearguard thwart Lech's efforts, their example inspired their midfield colleagues to a more composed game.

Thereafter Aberdeen always looked more likely to make the goal breakthrough and apart from Bell's goal, Gordon Strachan had what seemed a perfectly legitimate goal disallowed a few minutes before the final whistle.

Over the 90 minutes, Willie Miller and Alex McLeish were Aberdeen's outstanding players, while Doug Bell came close to challenging the defensive pair for the honour on his second-half performance.

Bell was booked just before the interval and a similar fate befell Poznan's Adamiec a few minutes earlier.

1983

SHERGAR, Margaret Thatcher, Thriller, Gandhi and Gothenburg. In and out of Aberdeen, the year of 1983 was packed with events which ensured it would linger long in the memory of everyone who lived through it. Whether in sport, politics, news, music or film there were landmark events in a 12 month period packed with highs and lows, joy and sorrow with so many headline grabbing moments remaining talking points quarter of a century later.

As Aberdonians brought in the New Year there was only a hint of what was in store for the city's football team, with the Dons through to the quarter-final stage at the turn of the year but far from favourites for the European crown which would soon be theirs. The more immediate concern for the north-east public at the beginning of 1983 was getting the better of the elements. Temperatures plummeted as treacherous snow drifts and biting winds enveloped the region. Vast swathes of the country were brought to a grinding halt as the authorities struggled to cope with road closures and a catalogue of accidents caused by the impossible conditions.

Aside from the march to football stardom, transport was at the centre of attention within the city in the opening months of the year. After the traffic chaos caused by the harsh weather, the Aberdeen bus service was radically shaken up in January as bus stops were moved and routes changed completely. The only problem was nobody had told the passengers, with the exception of some public advertising which apparently had gone unnoticed.

The travelling public were not amused and their humour took another turn for the worse in February of 1983 when Aberdeen City Council decided to controversially ban smoking on buses. Again the travelling public took stock, and the smokers opted to ignore the new rule and keep on puffing despite the new signs which had sprung up on every bus they travelled on. A total ban on smoking in public was not even on the agenda, especially after the outcry surrounding the bus ban.

Rail was the next service to make the news, with British Transport announcing in March that it was transferring the Station Hotel in Aberdeen, and the equivalent in Inverness, into private ownership. Britain was changing and the Granite City was moving with the times.

The business scene in the city had a new kid on the block in the shape of Aberdeen Fund Managers, set up by chartered accountant Martin Gilbert with just £20,000 of capital. Now transformed to Aberdeen Asset Management, the organisation has a worldwide profile and more than £95billion under its control. Gilbert has become one of Aberdeen's highest profile businessmen and is now a key member of the Dons board, with AAM holding a significant stake in the club.

On a smaller scale, other new businesses in the area included I&K Motors in Inverurie, which has gone on to become one of Scotland's largest car retailers, and the introduction of Under The Hammer to the Aberdeen pub scene. The Trinity Centre, which opened its doors in 1984 and unearthed a hoard of 4,500 medieval coins during construction in the winter of 1983, was in the pipeline and plans for the St Nicholas Centre, launched in 1985, were also on the drawing board.

The oil business was shaping up nicely in the industry's European capital, with three new fields approved in 1983 to take the total to 31. The figure is dwarfed by the 2007 total of 209 fields, demonstrating the enormous growth in the sector in the past 25 years, but it was still a major factor in everyday life in the north-east.

the average house price in 1983 was £29,000 in Scotland

That growth had helped the area thrive. As Aberdeen headed for Gothenburg they left behind a city which boasted a population of 214,400. The number of residents peaked at 219,880 in 1995 before dipping back towards 200,000 in recent years. In contrast, Aberdeenshire's population has risen from 192,000 at the time of Aberdeen FC's finest hour to close to 240,000 as more and more people swap the city for the shire. The average house price in 1983 was £29,000 in Scotland and £40,000 in London with the average male wage north of the border sitting at £146 per week.

The build-up to Gothenburg, and the long post-final celebrations embraced by Aberdonians, overshadowed the build-up to the 1983 general election. Margaret Thatcher and her Conservative party swept to victory, securing her second term in power with a greatly increased majority. The joy was tempered soon after when

Conservative chairman Cecil Parkinson tendered his resignation following his admission of an affair with a former secretary who was expecting his child. Thatcher's return to office was not the only significant development on the political scene that summer. The election had produced few shocks but one was the ousting of Hamish Gray in the Ross and Cromarty constituency. It had been a safe Tory seat but a young whippersnapper by the name of Charles Kennedy had upset the apple cart. Kennedy, the future Liberal Democrat leader, became the youngest MP at Westminster when he defeated Gray at the tender age of 22.

The football team's success had a huge impact on city life, with the feelgood factor sweeping the area and baking summer temperatures helping to maintain the carefree atmosphere. In fact the fleet of Grampian gritters, so busy during the first couple of months of the year, were forced back into action in June – when they were tasked with helping to prevent the region's roads from melting in the intense heat, with temperatures in the 80s causing tar to melt during the finest spell of weather since 1976.

Not everyone was impressed with what the north-east had to offer mind you, with American travel writer Paul Theroux stoking up flames of protest when he was highly critical of Aberdeen in his 1983 travel book 'The Kingdom by the Sea'. The book charted his journey around Britain's coast and he described the home of the Dons as "an awful city – quite the worst, most smug, self-centred place in Britain". Theroux, the

John Hewitt had become Hilton Academy's most famouse fp

father of quirky documentary maker Louis, was not welcome at the parties which sprung up following the homecoming of Alex Ferguson and his heroes.

In December 1983, Press and Journal columnist Norman Harper wrote: "As if victory in Gothenburg was not enough, the Dons confirmed their new super-status at the end of the year by trouncing the mighty Hamburg in the European Super Cup. Again, celebration was prolonged. Aberdeen stood at the top of the European club ladder – a place the city occupies yet. But for many, the true moment of glory will still be that sweet sound of the final whistle in Gothenburg in May. The glow is with us still. And who knows. If tourism in the north-east had been able to bottle the fun, frolic and spirit of that evening, they might not have had to try to persuade the world that haggis are alive and well and living in the wilds of Deeside."

There was no room for sentiment on the back of the Ullevi success though. John Hewitt had become Hilton Academy's most famous FP but that did not save his school from the threat of closure, with the issue first becoming public as 1983 drew to a close. The row rumbled on but the school did eventually close its doors.

The most significant news event in Aberdeen that year was as far removed from the joy of Gothenburg as could possibly be imagined. The city was hit by disaster.

On October 27 the Stakis owned Royal Darroch Hotel in Cults was ripped apart by an early morning gas explosion. The tragedy claimed six lives and left a trail of casualties. The horror of the events of that day haunted the suburb, which had Alex Ferguson as its most notable resident, and the area as a whole. Some guests had attempted to leap to safety from bedroom windows on the upper floors as fire took hold of the 67 bedroom luxury residence and the tragedy received international coverage. The hotel was never rebuilt, with the site transformed into a retirement complex.

Worldwide, the Americans completed their first space walk in nine years when the space shuttle Challenger made a successful maiden voyage. Among the crew was Sally Ride, the first female US astronaut.

In Britain, the first heart and transplant operation carried out in the United Kingdom was completed in London. It took a team of 20 doctors and nurses five hours to complete the surgery.

It was one of the few bright spots in world news in 1983, with the year filled by death and destruction. Showbusiness lost David Niven and Karen Carpenter but it was a series of conflicts across the globe which dominated the headlines.

In January tensions in Nigeria reached new levels when the country's government decided to force hundreds of immigrants from Ghana back to their homeland and in June there was panic in Sri Lanka as British tourists were told to flee from the island due to an outbreak of fighting between Sinhalese radicals and Tamils.

In September a Korean airliner, with 269 people on board, disappeared over the Soviet Pacific island of Sakhalin. Korean recordings showed it had been shot down by two Soviet fighter jets, although it took the Kremlin almost a week to admit its forces had acted after the pilot of the passenger plane had ignored repeated warnings to vacate Soviet airspace. Pilots around the world boycotted flights too and from the Soviet Union while Aeroflot, the USSR airline, was banned from western airports.

Other world news included the deaths of more than half of the South Korean cabinet in an explosion in Burma and a coup on the Caribbean island of Grenada which left Premier Maurice Bishop murdered. It led to US intervention, welcomed by islanders but criticised by Margaret Thatcher and her government.

The Middle East also saw continued troubles, despite the presence of UN peace keeping forces in Lebanon. The American embassy in Beirut was bombed with deadly consequence and 286 troops from the US and French forces died when guerrillas on kamikaze missions drove explosive laden trucks into their camps. Two American fighters were also shot down by Syria during a turbulent and bloody period.

Closer to home there were few happier tales. A group of 38 IRA prisoners escaped from the Maze Prison in September – only 11 were recaptured as the troubles on the Emerald Isle continued. Just before Christmas a car bomb exploded outside Harrods in London, killing six shoppers.

Terrorists were not the only individuals generating headlines in 1983. On January 13 two Scotland Yard detectives opened fire on a Mini which they believed was carrying David Martin, one of the country's most wanted men, but discovered the driver was an innocent young film editor called Steven Waldorf. He made a full recovery, the officers were not disciplined and Martin was later captured and sentenced to 25 years imprisonment.

In February, the quiet and introverted figure of Dennis Nilsen appeared in court in London to face a murder charge. It transpired he had committed one of the most gruesome crimes Britain had ever seen, luring young men back to his Muswell Hill flat before killing them, cutting up their bodies and boiling parts of them on a gas cooker. He was sentenced to 25 years for six murders and two attempted murders.

Man was not solely responsible for the woes of 1983, with mother nature proving Australia's enemy as, early in the year, bush fires ripped through Victoria and New South Wales during the worst drought the country had experienced in the 20th century.

In world politics, Helmut Kohl became chancellor of Germany. On home soil, the Labour party regrouped following the election of Neil Kinnock as their leader. His appointment came at a time when a concerted anti-nuclear campaign kicked off in Britain, in preparation for the arrival of the first Cruise missiles in November that year. Less controversial political moves were also taking hold in the UK. On January 31 the use of seatbelts in the front of all cars became compulsory as the Government attempted to combat road safety problems. Introducing the law was widely accepted as a sensible step forward but enforcing it proved problematic as drivers, set in their ways, proved difficult to convince.

Motorists had more choice than ever when deciding which car to belt themselves into. The much maligned Austrin Allegro ceased production to be replaced by the all singing, all dancing Maestro. For Vauxhall the new addition to the range was the Nova, which faced competition from Fiat's newly introduced Uno. The Uno was voted Europe's car of the year in 1984, with the Audi 100 winning the 83 title. Ford hoped to take the Escort upmarket with the introduction of the four-door Orion version of its popular model while the Datsun name was about to disappear completely to be replaced by the Nissan tag.

Cabbage Patch Kids were unleashed for the first time

It was also possible to stay in touch while behind the wheel too. In 1983 the grandson of Alexander Graham Bell answered the first ever commercial mobile phone call to mark the start of a new era in communication.

The Apple Lisa was the big breakthrough in the computer world. The new machine was the first to allow users to interact with their PC using graphics, the first, if very basic, attempt at a Windows style set-up.

The phrase 'virtual reality' was first used in 1983 as the new passion for technology moved ahead at pace while more practical inventions included the first soft bifocal contact lens.

The world of toys had a new craze as Cabbage Patch Kids were unleashed for the first time. They became the most successful doll ever introduced as millions flew off the shelves in stores across the globe.

The other must-have for British children was less expensive, with Cadbury launching the Wispa bar in 1983. The advertising campaign used John Thaw and Dennis Waterman from The Sweeney and and Hi De Hi duo Simon Cadell and Ruth Madoc.

As Wispa arrived on sweet shop counters, packets of Space Dust disappeared. The popping candy was a victim of an urban myth that eating it and drinking Coca-Cola at the same time would cause the 'victim's' stomach to explode. Yes, 1983 was also the year of the gullible youth.

Consumers were beginning to regain confidence in time for the wave of new products. The Conservatives were on an economic drive, with inflation dropping to 3.7% in 1983. The other major monetary move was more tangible, with the introduction of the £1 coin on April 20.

The coin, which was not universally accepted by the public, was not the only long lasting new arrival. In Japan, Disneyland Tokyo was launched in the spring of 1983 and within five weeks 1million visitors had passed through the gates. It had taken 23 years to turn the Disney dream into reality in the Far East.

the compact disc was also officially launched in the year of Aberdeen's triumph in Gothenburg

The compact disc was also officially launched in the year of Aberdeen's triumph in Gothenburg. CDs were dismissed by record collectors as little more than a fad but in the 25 years since their introduction more than 200 billion have sold worldwide. The first disc was actually manufactured in 1982 by Philips in Germany, having been co-developed with Sony, and the landmark production was a copy of The Visitors by Abba. The first 150 CD titles went to the Japanese market before the new medium's introduction to European shores in March the following year.

The most popular song, primarily on vinyl, when Willie Miller stepped forward to lift the European Cup Winners' Cup was True by Spandau Ballet. It held the No.1 spot in the British chart on May 11. The other, albeit minor, pop event on May 11 was the birth of one-hit Australian wonder Holly Valance in 1983.

Far more notable was the release of Michael Jackson's epic Thriller video. The multi-million dollar effort was the work of Hollywood director John Landis and a truly groundbreaking moment in the music industry.

In Aberdeen, music fans were treated to a date on U2's War tour at the Capitol Theatre in February in the days when the Union Street venue, now the Chicago Rock theme bar, was one of the UK's foremost hosts of live music.

U2 were not among the bands responsible for the 18 number one songs in 1983. They included Down Under by Men at Work, Too Shy by Kajagoogoo, Bonnie Tyler's hit Total Eclipse of the Heart, Let's Dance by David Bowie, Every Breath You Take by the Police, Michael Jackson's chart topping Billie Jean, Red Red Wine by UB40, Uptown Girl by Billy Joel, Karma Chameleon by Culture Club and Relax by Frankie Goes to Hollywood. The Eurovision song contest title went to Luxembourg.

In film, Richard Attenborough's production of Gandhi set a new British record when it won a staggering eight Oscars. Other popular releases at the cinemas included Educating Rita, The Big Chill starring Kevin Kline, Glenn Close and Jeff Goldblum and Woody Allen's hit Zelig. With a more tartan tinge, the cult film Local Hero was released in the same year set against the stunning north-east backdrop of Pennan.

The art world in Scotland was cheered in 1983 when the Burrell Collection in Glasgow finally opened at its permanent home in Pollok Country Park. It had been agreed in 1963 that it was the perfect location but it took two decades to design and complete the centre.

On the small screen, Aberdeen had another reason to celebrate success in 1983 when Grampian Television presenter Selina Scott was recruited to join the team for the launch of a new concept: breakfast television. From Yorkshire but with Aberdeen grandparents, Scott was co-host for the BBC with Frank Bough for Britain's first ever attempt at the genre – and she even donned an Aberdeen scarf on the morning after the night before in Gothenburg.

In comedy, Blackadder was beginning to create waves and Blockbusters presented a new and innovative television quiz format which captured the imagination of a nation.

The television companies did not just give to their viewers in 1983, they took away too. After a six year run the Professionals was brought to an end in the year of Gothenburg and Terry Wogan's tenure as host of Blankety Blank also concluded.

The television schedules had a new kid on the block for the New Year, with Channel 4 launched in the final weeks of 1982 to add to the existing three options. The BBC offered daytime delights such as Pebble Mill and Play School while the evening schedule featured Bergerac and Taxi. Miss World remained a firm TV fixture and in 1983 there was a British winner in the shape of Dorset's Sarah-Jane Hutt.

Radio 1's breakfast show was in the hands of Mike Read, who kept the studio warm for daytime presenters Simon Bates, Mike Smith, Steve Wright and Peter Powell. Across the dial on Radio 2, Terry Wogan was the early man with the likes of Jimmy Young and Gloria Hunniford also on the studio list.

Celebrity in 1983 was not restricted to television, radio and film stars though, an animal also got in on the act in the most unfortunate and mysterious circumstances. In February the Irish stable of Derby winner Shergar was raided and the horse disappeared into the night before a £2million ransom demand was made. The kidnappers later dropped their demand to £40,000 for a stallion valued at £10million but the syndicate who owned Shergar refused to pay, hoping to deter repeats in the future.

They called the bluff of the group who had carried out the crime, with at least six men believed to have been involved, but it did not lead to the return of their prize asset. The distinctive horse has never been found and insurers paid out more than £7million to the stable which had been owned by the Aga Khan and his family for more than six decades.

The other equally famous crime of the year occurred in London on a November morning. The Brink's-Mat robbery at Heathrow netted an armed gang £26 million in gold. A bribed security guard let the six man team into the company's warehouse at the airport. They poured petrol over staff and threatened them with a lit match if they did not reveal the combination numbers of the vault. More than £17m of the money realised from the gold has been accounted for by police but some of the remainder is thought to have been invested in property in Britain and Spain. Dozens of gold bars are still unaccounted for and only two of the robbers have been convicted. Michael McAvoy and Brian Robinson were sentenced to 25 years.

Amid the crime, death and destruction it was left to sport to lighten the mood.

Aberdeen's European double made headlines across the continent while in England it was Liverpool who dominated the league

Aberdeen's European double made headlines across the continent while in England it was Liverpool who dominated the league and Manchester United who claimed the FA Cup.

Significantly for Scotland's international future, the venue for the 1986 World Cup was changed in 1983 when it became clear Columbia would not be able to stage the tournament as planned. Instead it was Mexico who were awarded the right to host the competition.

The Mexico finals were a distant dream for the national side, who in 1983 were engrossed in their qualifying bid for Euro 84 under Jock Stein. Results included a 2-2 against Switzerland, a 1-1 draw against Belgium and a 2-1 defeat against East Germany. The bid to qualify for the finals in France failed.

In the home internationals Scotland lost 2-0 against Northern Ireland and fell to the same score against England but managed to beat Wales 2-0 and draw 0-0 with Northern Ireland in the first of two contests between the two countries that year. In the success against the Welsh it was Andy Gray and Alan Brazil who scored long before Sky television or Talksport radio had joined the broadcasting scene.

In the year Aberdeen supporters earned a glowing reputation on the continent, England's followers were not covering themselves in the same type of glory. Twenty were arrested in Luxembourg for fighting and stealing on the night their national team defeated the hosts but still failed to qualify for Euro 84.

The Open golf championship was won by Tom Watson at Royal Birkdale but there was European success in The Masters as the charismatic Seve Ballesteros swept to the green jacket. Hal Sutton, the leading money winner on the US PGA Tour in 1983, won the PGA Championship while Larry Nelson took the honours in the US Open.

It was also a Ryder Cup year, with the PGA National course at Palm Beach in Florida providing the sun soaked setting for golf's biggest team event. The Americans defeated Europe 14 ½-13 ½ and it was a nail biting tournament, with Europe coming within touching distance of a landmark first win on US soil. The European team, featuring Sam Torrance in the British contingent, was captained by Englishman Tony Jacklin while Jack Nicklaus led the opposition.

Steve Davis was snooker's world champion after defeating Cliff Thornburn and the

most importantly Britain also had the kings of Europe on the football field

Wimbledon singles titles went to John McEnroe and Martina Navratilova. The BBC sports personality of the year award went to Steve Cram on the back of his 1500m victory over world record holder Steve Ovett in the inaugural World Championship as the preparations for the 1984 Olympics in Los Angeles gathered pace.

Larry Holmes and Michael Dokes defended their heavyweight boxing titles while in the highest profile bout of 1983 there was success for Marvin Hagler in retaining his unified world middleweight title by defeating Roberto Duran.

Britain had its own world champions to covet … in ice dancing, with Jayne Torvill and Christopher Dean skating to victory.

Most importantly Britain also had the kings of Europe on the football field. Aberdeen Football Club, the real heroes of 1983.

● The Aberdeen players are able to smile after being paired with German stars Bayern Munich in the quarter-finals. Pictured, from left, back row: John Hewitt, Willie Miller, Stuart Kennedy, Gordon Strachan, Neil Simpson, Eric Black, Doug Rougvie. Front: Alex McLeish, Neale Cooper.

QUARTER-FINAL FIRST LEG, BAYERN MUNICH v ABERDEEN
MARCH 2, 1983: BAYERN MUNICH 0 , ABERDEEN 0

WHEN Aberdeen were paired with Bayern Munich in the quarter finals the Dons and their supporters had a full four months to let the enormity of the task sink in. After the victory against Lech Poznan at the start of November 1982, the competition was paused until early March 1983.

Normally it would have given Alex Ferguson a perfect opportunity for reconnaissance but the six week winter break in German domestic football hampered the spying mission.

Not that the Pittodrie coaching staff had to look too far for information on an opposition team packed full of household names. Before the start of the 1982/83 season the German giants had shelled out £1million on new talent to augment the batch of superstars they already possessed, with the spending expedition the result of a third place finish in the Bundesliga.

When Aberdeen touched down in Munich for the first leg at the awe inspiring Olympic Stadium they did so with the aim of becoming the first foreign team ever to defeat Bayern on their own patch in European competition. The only side to triumph in the continental cups in Munich in 55 ties prior to Aberdeen's visit was Eintracht Frankfurt in the 1978 Uefa Cup with a 2-1 win.

Bayern will certainly know they have been in a game

Ferguson insisted the venue would work in his side's favour, claiming: "Aberdeen are always at their best on big, wide open pitches. The Olympic Stadium suits us right down to the ground. It is impressive and probably enough to take the breath away from an unsuspecting player – but our finest performances have come on sprawling grounds such as Parkhead, Ibrox and Hampden."

Aberdeen arrived in Germany high on confidence, having won 11 of their last 12 domestic games, but faced a side full of experience. Bayern's average age was 27, contrasted against the Dons average of 24, and with several Munich players entering the twilight of their career the intention for Ferguson was to ensure his side kept the tempo high.

Ferguson told the press he would settle for a 2-0 defeat in Munich and still be confident of going through by winning by a greater margin at Pittodrie in the return game. His side did far better than that, answering their manager's pre-match challenge of "We've got to find out how good we really are" by matching the German stars every step of the way and emerging with a 0-0 draw that made European football stand up and take notice.

Bayern had overcome Tottenham Hotspur 5-1 over two legs in the previous round and Spurs manager Keith Burkinshaw had hailed the Bundesliga men as "one of the finest technical sides I have come across".

World Cup heroes Paul Breitner and Karl Heinz Rummenigge were the highest profile names in the side, worlds apart financially from their Dons counterparts with Breitner paid £40,000 simply to shave his beard off by an aftershave firm in 1982 while Rummenigge had signed a £375,000 per year contract in the build-up to the Aberdeen match.

Rummenigge, Udo Horsmann and Bernd Durnberger all survived from the European Cup final win against St Etienne at Hampden in 1976 while cultured defender Klaus Augenthaler, an international star in the making, was one of the emerging talents for Bayern.

The eager young Dons were not daunted despite crashing out of European competition against German opposition in three of the four previous campaigns. Captain Willie Miller was the only survivor from all six of those ties but he went into the Munich game with his chest puffed out, warning: "We have learned from those mistakes and Bayern will certainly know they have been in a game."

And so it transpired, with the goalless draw in Munich giving Aberdeen a platform to go on an claim a berth in the semi-finals of the famous tournament. Miller did not have it all his own way, losing a tooth in his battle with Rummenigge in the first leg.

Ferguson's pre-match opinion that he would settle for a one or two goal defeat had shifted considerably by the end of the first leg. As he boarded the return flight to Scotland, the manager said: "Bayern were there to be beaten – my only regret is that we didn't grab a goal when the opportunity was there. The tie is by no means over, in fact the hardest part has still to come as we must now beat Bayern at Pittodrie."

● The travelling Dons party prepare to board the club's chartered plane at Aberdeen Airport ahead of the quarter-final tie in Munich.

DONS KEEP EURO FLAG FLYING

German stars mastered at their own game

MUNICH'S Olympic Stadium was a magnificently fitting backdrop for Aberdeen's greatest triumph in 15 years of European football.

In this their 45th game in the European cup competitions, the Dons took on triple European Cup winners Bayern Munich and emerged as the more competent combine, making a mockery of pre-match forecasts in the Southern German city that Bayern would win by something like a five goal margin.

Aberdeen's task in their bid to qualify for the semi-final of the European Cup Winners' Cup is still far from completed, but surely they have accomplished the major part of it by taking the tie to the second leg at Pittodrie still on level terms with their German opponents.

Aberdeen's planning for this match was thorough, and it certainly paid off as every member of the side played his part in what, despite the score line, was a moral victory.

For long spells the Dons beat their hosts at their own game will cool, composed precision football.

Although the Germans had marginally more shots at goal than the Dons in the first half,

BAYERN MUNICH	0
ABERDEEN	0

● Miller and Kennedy thwart Bayern

almost all these tries came from a range of 25 yards or more, and with Jim Leighton holding everything that came his way with supreme confidence there was no real threat to the Aberdeen goal.

The Dons in fact came closer to scoring in the opening 45 minutes and Bayern were relieved when goalkeeper Manfred Muller turned net-bound shots from Peter Weir and Mark McGhee away for corners.

The longer the game went on the more composed the Aberdeen team became, and such was their control of the proceedings that

manager Alex Ferguson was able to introduce Gordon Strachan as a substitute for Eric Black with 14 minutes to go, too short a time for the midfield international to make any impact on the game but a valuable piece of match practice for him after a five-game absence.

The Aberdeen players were heroes all, but a special word of praise is due to skipper Willie Miller, who not only provided the inspirational leadership which has come to b expected from him, but also achieved the rare feat of subduing one of the most dangerous strikers in world football in Karl-Heinz Rummenige to the extent that the West German international skipper showed only rare flashes of his ability.

With Neale Cooper performing a similar function in his policing of Paul Breitner, the two danger men of the Bayern side were reduced to near impotency.

The greatest danger in the Bayern attack came from Karl Del'Haye. This small tricky player, operating on the Bayern right touch line, gave Doug Rougvie a less than comfortable evening, but the big full back stuck manfully to his task and finally put a halter on his opponent.

FOOTBALL

LEIGHTON was the first keeper to handle the ball – from a passback – but it was the Dons who launched the opening raid.

Rummenigge gave an early indication of his danger when he almost managed to slip between McLeish and Miller as Leighton moved of his line to retrieve the ball.

Miller showed that the Aberdeen defence meant business with a crunching tackle on Kraus in four minutes. The Bayern midfield man required attention and from the subsequent free kick Augenthaler sent a raging 30-yard shot just wide.

Aberdeen were having a fair share of the game territorially in the opening stages but the Germans were lightning fast on the break and equally quick to shoot on sight of goal.

Nachtweih sent a try wide of Leighton's right hand post on one such occasion.

The Aberdeen keeper was clutching the cross balls with great confidence.

Miller started an Aberdeen attack with a break forward in 11 minutes. The Aberdeen skipper found Weir on the left and the move ended with Bell having a shot blocked by a massed Bayern defence.

Five minutes later Weir brought out a full length diving save from Muller, who only just managed to fingertip the ball round his lefthand upright.

● Leighton in action against Karl-Heinze Rummenigge

The Dons early play had their supporters in good voice, but at one stage the chant "Come on you Reds" faded into embarrassed silence on the realisation that it was the Bayern side who were wearing red on this occasion, the Dons being clad in white shirts and black shorts.

In 22 minutes a 60-yard dash by Große from deep in the Bayern defence ended in anticlimax when his parting shot was well wide of goal.

A minute later Nachtweih did get the ball on target, but Leighton got his body behind the fierce grounder from 20 yards.

Augenthaler again moved up on a free kick 10 yards outside the Aberdeen penalty box in 31 minutes but this time it was Breitner who took the kick, side-footing the ball to Augenthaler whose low shot was well saved by

the alert Leighton.

Four minutes later an Aberdeen break on the right saw Kennedy get in a cross but the ball bounced agonisingly over Black's head as the young striker leapt to meet the ball with only the goalkeeper to beat.

The Bayern goal had the narrowest escape of the game in 36 minutes when Muller did well to turn an angled shot from McGhee away from his goal, the ball going just wide of his right hand post.

The Dons were certainly giving their more experienced opponents something to think about, and there were signs that the Bayern supporters were becoming impatient with their team as the interval approached.

McGhee brought out another save from Muller in 40 minutes and when Bayern broke away in retaliation Horsmann finished wildly, sending a 20 yard shot well wide of target.

A wayward crossfield pass by Del'Haye, which Kennedy was quick to seize upon, saw Aberdeen mount the first attack of the second half but the move floundered when the full back's cross was intercepted by Horsmann.

The Dons maintained the pressure and Black just failed to make contact when he threw himself at Weir's cross in 5 minutes.

Bayern returned to the offensiv

Eric Black beats the Bayern defence to the ball

Miller and Leighton were [ ] to concede a corner to tidy up [ ]tentially nasty situation in the [ ]rdeen goalmouth. Then [ ]ghton dived to save a [ ]mmenigge header from a [ ]mmier cross.

Spanish referee lectured [ ]per for a challenge on [ ]'Haye. The blonde winger was [ ]ping for a few minutes after [ ]ming, following on-the-field [ ]tment.

[ ] Bayern team's concern at the [ ] the match was going was [ ]ayed in a number of the [ ]mans' passes going astray.

[ ]y a reflex save by Leighton [ ]rted disaster for Aberdeen in [ ]minutes. Rummenigge held off [ ]iller challenge long enough to get in a shot on the turn but Leighton dived to push the ball away for a corner.

The Bayern raids were becoming more infrequent and when the Munich side did attack in force they were foiled by a composed Aberdeen defence.

To the cheers of jubilant Dons supporters Gordon Strachan made an appearance in 76 minutes when he replaced Black.

It was Leighton to the rescue again when Groβe sent in a 35-yard drive a minute later.

Miller was injured in a goalmouth clash of heads with Rummenigge, but the hardy Aberdeen skipper recovered before play was interrupted.

Augenthaler gave an indication of Bayern's frustration in the venom with which he booted the ball away for a corner in an Aberdeen raid in 84 minutes.

The big sweeper, however, was quick to break forward a minute later. Once again Leighton brought off a fine save from the Bayern defender's 25-yard drive.

BAYERN MUNICH – Muller, Dremmler, Horsmann, Groβe, Augenthaler, Kraus, Nachtweih, Breitner, Hoeness, Del'Haye, Rummenigge.

ABERDEEN – Leighton, Kennedy, Rougvie, Cooper, McLeish, Miller, Black (Strachan), Simpson, McGhee, Bell, Weir.

Referee – E. C. Guruceta Muro, Spain.

ALEX FERGUSON PROFILE

I **AM** looking forward to a long and happy stay here. With those words, Alex Ferguson announced his arrival as the new manager of Aberdeen Football Club on the first day of June in 1978.

Nobody could have predicted just how much joy the next eight years would bring for the freshly appointed coach and his Red Army. He was 35 at the time, not long retired from playing and determined to carve out a career to support his wife and three young sons.

He sold his two pubs in Glasgow and the family home in East Kilbride to throw himself into the new challenge at Pittodrie, moving the Ferguson clan lock stock and barrel to their new base in Cults.

He had first been linked with the top job at Aberdeen in the summer of 1977 following Ally MacLeod's departure but his club St Mirren acted quickly, tabling a new four year contract, and it was Billy McNeill who took charge of the Dons.

One year later it was all change again, with McNeill heading for Celtic and the Ferguson link finally becoming reality. The circumstances, to say the least, were controversial. Although Ferguson had been considered a contender for the Aberdeen vacancy he still had three years of his Saints contract to run and that had deterred the prudent Pittodrie board from making an approach.

Their counterparts in the Love Street board room made it easy for them, sensationally sacking Ferguson on 30 May 1978 citing breach of contract. Two days later he was installed as the new manager of Aberdeen.

The messy details of Ferguson's departure from Paisley were soon played out at an industrial tribunal following his claim for unfair dismissal. The young manager's practice of claiming £25 weekly expenses, which were tax free, were at the centre of the club's case despite the admission it was sanctioned by the chairman. Disputes over bonus payments to players were also raised amid a long list of petty arguments and Ferguson lost his claim against the club. Despite the ruling, Aberdeen stood steadfastly behind their new recruit and were convinced they had unearthed a gem of a coach who had fire in his belly and a desperate determination to make a go of his fledgling career in the dugout.

Dons chairman Dick Donald had developed a habit of choosing the right men to lead his beloved team. Eddie Turnbull was widely acknowledged as a manager far ahead of his time, Ally MacLeod had been head hunted by Scotland and Billy McNeill cherry picked by Celtic. For any young coach, it was obvious that Pittodrie had the potential to

● Alex Ferguson is held
aloft by Peter Weir (left) and
Doug Rougvie after the
Gothenburg triumph in 1983

make you a star and the latest incumbent planned to grab his opportunity with both hands.

It emerged during the tribunal that Ferguson had agreed to take a pay cut to move to the north-east, with his salary dropping from a basic £15,000 at St Mirren to £14,000 with the Dons, with a top of the range club Rover car to help bridge the gap. Generous bonuses were on offer if he could lead the club to success and in the fullness of time that element of the deal came into full force as the manager landed trophy after trophy, providing unprecedented value for money. Even the thrifty Aberdeen board could not grudge signing the cheques which represented yet more success for their cherished team.

As he was introduced to the press on his first day at Pittodrie, the new manager said: "Aberdeen is a fine club with excellent facilities. I know there is a good squad of players at Pittodrie but there is still a big challenge for me here. I'm a winner by nature and I want to win things for Aberdeen Football Club."

There was no case of the new broom sweeping clear. Ferguson, a man not renowned for his patience, took time to assess what he had inherited and was measured in his efforts to put his own stamp on the Dons side. He was pleasantly surprised by his initial dealings with a pool of players who proved eager to impress and committed to his vision for the club.

Within his first two weeks the manager was predicting a bright future, prophetically he even claimed during the 1978 pre-season that success in Europe was not beyond the realms of possibility. Ferguson said: "What has impressed me most is the attitude of the players. Like myself, they are desperate to get started and I was very pleased to hear the players who popped in for a bit of advance training and a chat speaking about going for the treble. That's the attitude I want at Pittodrie and I reckon that with a fair share of the breaks we will be knocking at the door. I can only repeat that I am delighted to be manager and am hungry for success.

"It's equally clear that the club directors are just as ambitious as the players. The fact that Pittodrie is Britain's first all-seated stadium is just one indication. I am very keen for us to have a good run in Europe for both the fans and Scottish football in general. Too often our teams topple at the fist hurdle and the spectators deserve better. It is essential that we step up our game. If the players adopt the right approach and increase their game then we could do quite well."

It took five years of hard graft and careful planning, but that bold prediction did come true for a manager on a mission. Ferguson became renowned as the most driven coach in the country, leaving no stone unturned in his pursuit of perfection and not afraid to cause waves when necessary. He fostered a 'them against us' attitude for his east coast team, not shy of claiming west coast bias in the media and even within the game's governing body. On more than one occasion he went toe to toe with the SFA to defend his players, he was an adopted Aberdonian and prepared to fight his team and his city's corner.

That approach was at odds with Ferguson's background - he was as west coast as they came, steeped in the history and heritage of the Govan shipyards where his father grafted.

He did, however, have to leave Glasgow behind to earn his break in football. Ferguson was a schoolboy, youth and amateur international before joining St Johnstone from Queen's Park in 1960. He switched to Dunfermline four years later and in 1967 Rangers paid in excess of £60,000 to lure him back to Glasgow. He went on to play for Falkirk and Ayr United before moving into management.

Ferguson, who had been appointed player coach at Falkirk at the start of 1973, had started the 1974/75 season in charge at lowly East Stirling. He had to be cajoled to take on one of Scottish football's least glamorous roles but set about the task with vigour and was highly thought of by the Firs Park board.

The relationship was brief, with St Mirren stepping in on the recommendation of former Rangers figurehead Willie Waddell to snap up the emerging managerial talent. The part-time Paisley outfit had gone through a staggering 11 managers in 10 years but the new man, not short of confidence despite his lack of experience, believed he could stop the rot.

His approach was radical, with Ferguson clearing the decks by releasing 19 players after taking charge. He turned out to be a solid judge of a player even in the infancy of his coaching days, with not one of the 19 freed squad members staying in the senior game after being axed by the rookie boss. There was no fear or trepidation as he set about the task of rebuilding the Paisley Saints and reputations meant nothing as he relentlessly pursued a root and branch operation.

Ferguson, had instigated the creation of a new youth policy in his stint at East Stirling and repeated the exercise at St Mirren, doubling the number of boys teams within the structure. The Buddies young guns won Scottish Cup titles at under-15 and under-16 level in the creator's final season as he set about searching for the cream of Scottish talent. More often than not he found himself in competition with bigger clubs, including Aberdeen, as his scouting network grew and he had no qualms about moving into rival territory, such as the north-east, to scout for fresh blood.

More importantly, he got results with the senior team. Promoted from the First

Division to the top flight under Ferguson, the Love Street side won a reputation for a cavalier approach to the game and attendances soared.

In made him an appealing and enduring choice for Aberdeen when it came to choosing McNeill's replacement. Commercially and in football terms he was the ideal candidate to fulfil the potential the Pittodrie board was so convinced their club possessed. Ferguson had been assisted by former Rangers team-mate Davie Provan at St Mirren but Pat Stanton was the coach he chose as his right hand man at Pittodrie as he threw himself into the role in wholehearted fashion following his arrival in the summer of 1978.

The first season went from the joy of his appointment to despair for the new man within months, with Ferguson losing his father early in 1979. In football, his team finished fourth in the league and runners-up in the League Cup but far happier days were just round the corner.

the Dons surged forward in the league during a season in which they beat Celtic a hat-trick of times and recorded five league and cup victories against Rangers

The 1979/80 season brought the league championship to Aberdeen, even though in the first two months of the campaign there was a threat that Ferguson could have been lured back to St Mirren after a boardroom reshuffle at Love Street. He was in demand, but the Dons manager was steadfast in his desire to remain at Pittodrie and guide the club to glory – the speculation about a Buddies return was killed stone dead by the manager and chairman Dick Donald.

The campaign had got off to an inauspicious start and a 3-0 defeat to Dundee United in the League Cup final replay in December 1979 did little to inspire hope that the manager's optimism, in the face of some faltering performances, about the success which lay ahead was justified.

Not for the first time and not for the last, Ferguson was proved right. The Dons surged forward in the league during a season in which they beat Celtic a hat-trick of times and recorded five league and cup victories against Rangers. The old guard was changing, with the Dons pipping the Hoops to the title in 1980 to become the first club outside of the Glasgow duo to win the Premier Division.

The 1980/81 term was fruitless, with Aberdeen finishing runners-up in the league just as they did the following season. In 1982 Ferguson did lift his second trophy with the reds, steering the team to the Scottish Cup in May that year. It was significant not just because it was a new prize to the boss but also because it came three months after the first real test of his commitment to the cause.

In the opening weeks of 1982 there was an approach from Wolverhampton Wanderers and Ferguson travelled to the Midlands for talks. The previous year Sheffield United had been given short shrift when they made a similar move but Wolves, who were prepared to make the Glaswegian the highest paid Scotsman in football management, were given a chance to state their case.

The outcome was swift and decisive, with Ferguson proclaiming: "I have turned them down, I'm staying at Pittodrie. There were one or two reasons but I really feel that the potential here at Aberdeen is not even half fulfilled. I believe so much in the players at Pittodrie and what they can achieve in the game. The potential is magnificent and if the players believe in themselves as much as I believe in them, there's no telling what we could do. One of the other main reasons was that the Aberdeen directors and fans have been good to me. Aberdeen is a good club to be with.

"Money does not compensate for doing the right thing – and maybe letting people down. Obviously I knew they would offer me great money, and it was great money in all aspects of it. But I don't want to talk about money as money wasn't my concern. I didn't want to let anyone down. Wolves are one of the best clubs in England and their tradition is unbelievable. I was pleased they came for me and the timing of their move means that I was their first choice. But I had to decide if I was doing the right thing – and I don't believe I have fulfilled my capacity as manager of Aberdeen."

Ferguson would not only have lined his pockets by moving to Molineux, he could also have cut his working hours in half. His talks with Wolves revealed that the football operation closed down at lunch time each day, a complete contradiction to the ethic he had instilled at Pittodrie. Once the first team squad finished their work in the morning, the Dons reserves and youth players were put through their paces in an afternoon session before the coaching session turned their attention to floodlit training with schoolboy signings in the evening.

It was all part of Ferguson's vision for the development of the club and a steady stream of home-grown players were already filtering through to the first team.

His decision to stay true to the club paved the way for the unprecedented success of the 1982/83 season, with the Scottish Cup joining the European Cup Winners' Cup on a rapidly expanding managerial cv.

It also sparked what was becoming an annual battle to retain the services of their conductor for the Dons directors. The winter of 1983, as the dust settled on the Gothenburg scenes of jubilation, brought the sternest test for the board they had faced in Ferguson's tenure up to that point.

John Greig had walked away from the Rangers manager's job and the Ibrox powerbrokers were casting envious eyes in the direction of the Granite City.

Ferguson's career as a Rangers player in his native Govan had not been a roaring success but he had the opportunity to exorcise those ghosts by returning as the main man. The inevitable approach was made to a manager who had chosen to work without a contract since arriving five years previously and there was an anxious wait for everyone connected with Aberdeen.

Then, on November 2 in 1983, the Evening Express headline screamed out 'Fergie says: I'm staying'. It was official, the pull of the team he watched as a boy and played for as a young professional was not enough to drag him away from his adopted home on the east coast.

Ferguson revealed: "I am with the club I want to be with. I have made the right decision, there's no doubt in my mind at all about that."

Chairman Dick Donald was at his manager's side as the landmark announcement was made, together with news of a five year contract which would tie Ferguson to the Dons until 1988.

Donald said: "The club under Alex Ferguson's leadership can continue to progress at the highest level in Scottish and European football. We have fought long and hard to retain our outstanding manager and now it has been worthwhile. I publicly thank Mr Ferguson for his cooperation in everything we have done. What was important to us was that we wanted him to stay."

The decision was a message of intent for the Dons players too. Alex McLeish said: "If Rangers or Celtic had said they were interested in a player or manager around five or six years ago then I think it is fair to say that they would have wanted to go. There would have been no sleepless nights or any dawn pacing of the living room floor searching for a decision. They would have wanted to go. But that picture has been steadily changing over the last few years and I'm sure the manager's decision will be a

major influence when it comes to discussing fresh contracts at the end of the season."
The five year deal was reputed to be worth anything up to £250,000 over its duration,
a far cry from the terms he joined the club on. Ferguson's stock was rising with every
trophy success and he was not finished yet.

The 1983/84 season, interrupted by the interest from Rangers, ended with Aberdeen as champions once again and with the Scottish Cup resting back at Pittodrie alongside the European Super Cup.

There was no respite for the Pittodrie directors in the summer of 1984 though, with Tottenham Hotspur the latest club to pursue the man at the top. Once again, Ferguson rejected a lucrative offer and told the Londoners to

> **n Hogmanay in 1984 the Dons manager's contribution to the game was recognised when he was awarded an OBE**

look elsewhere. He said: "Spurs made me a marvellous offer and I was impressed by
their chairman, but I have been preaching loyalty to my players and have decided to stay.
If I ever move, it will be for the challenge. Tottenham are capable of becoming the
biggest team in English football and I'm sure they will succeed whoever they appoint –
but I rejected them because I genuinely believe I am already with Britain's best."

As the 1984/85 season began it was confirmed that Ferguson has been appointed
second in command to Scotland manager Jock Stein, a role which would run in tandem
to his club job. He declined the assistant manager's title, preferring to be known simply
as a coach to the national team.

On hogmanay in 1984 the Dons manager's contribution to the game was recognised
when he was awarded an OBE in the New Year's honours list and the celebrations
continued well beyond January 1. In May 1985 the Premier Division was won again,
Ferguson completing a hat-trick of titles with the club.

He took the opportunity after seven years with the Dons to pen the first volume of his
memoirs, A Light in the North. The book, which was written by Ferguson without the
traditional aid of a ghostwriter, was an instant hit and the initial print run of 10,000
copies sold out as an adoring public clamoured to discover the secret to his success.

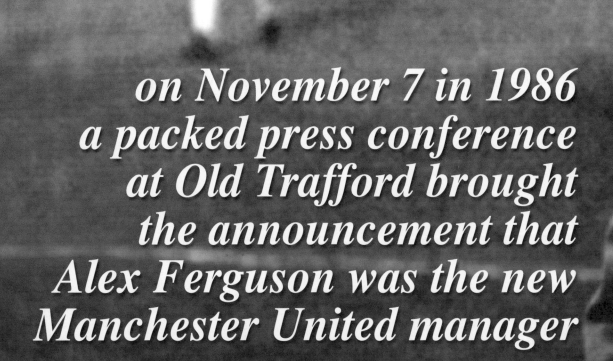

*on November 7 in 1986
a packed press conference
at Old Trafford brought
the announcement that
Alex Ferguson was the new
Manchester United manager*

The sales went on and on, sailing past 25,000 copies and making it a best seller. The start of the 1985/86 season proved tragic, with Stein's death during Scotland's match against Wales sending shockwaves throughout the game. Ferguson had viewed the legendary former Celtic boss as a father figure and was plunged into mourning at a time when he had to shoulder the burden of taking control of the national team during such a turbulent time.

He responded manfully, steadying the ship and helping to clinch qualification to the 1986 World Cup finals in Mexico where he remained in charge of Scotland. He had travelled to Mexico on the back of a successful club campaign which had brought a League Cup and Scottish Cup double for Aberdeen.

Ferguson was 43 when he answered the call from the SFA

Ferguson said: "I am not using this position with the national team to promote myself into another club job or secure the Scotland appointment on a permanent basis and the Aberdeen chairman Dick Donald understands this. I'll be eternally grateful to Mr Donald for giving me the chance to try to combine the two jobs. He could easily have turned down the SFA request for my services. There is no way I'm going to be leaving Aberdeen at present. There is a continuity there and I'm settled there. I have been seven and a half years with the Dons and I could stay for another seven and a half years."

Ferguson was 43 when he answered the call from the SFA. He was still a young manager but there was never any question about his ability to handle the pressure on the biggest football stage of all, or his ability to juggle the commitments of club and country. In fact, his talents had even sparked attention from the continent but Inter Milan, at the tail end of 1985, became the latest club in a long line to have the door slammed in their face when they tried to land the prize catch.

In Mexico the usual sky high expectations of the Tartan Army were tempered, with Ferguson's team drawing 0-0 with Uruguay before losing 2-1 to West Germany and 1-0 to Denmark. Jim Leighton was joined by Willie Miller, Alex McLeish and Gordon Strachan as the serving Dons who played in the finals.

On his return to club business, there was a radical move in the pipeline. In June 1986 Archie Knox, who had succeeded Pat Stanton as assistant manager at Aberdeen before departing to take charge of Dundee in 1983, returned as co-manager. It led to the departure of Willie Garner, who had stepped in to take on the assistant's role following Knox's move to Dens Park.

It gave the Red Army renewed hope for the new season, with the Gothenburg dream team reunited in the dug out, but the feel good factor would soon be well and truly shattered. The end of the most fantastic era was approaching.

On November 7 in 1986 a packed press conference at Old Trafford brought the announcement that Alex Ferguson was the new Manchester United manager. He claimed it was the only club in the world which would have tempted him to leave behind everything he had built in Scotland.

with Aberdeen I managed to break the Old Firm domination

Ferguson, who had been appointed as a director by Aberdeen just weeks earlier, said: "It is incredible to think that a club of United's size have not won a league championship in 20 years. That is a great challenge to me. With Aberdeen I managed to break the Old Firm domination, so that has to be my aim when it comes to the teams dominating in England. It was a wrench to leave such a beautiful place as Aberdeen."

United chairman Martin Edwards had secured the services of a coach who had an incredible list of honours against his name. Three league championships, the Scottish Cup four times, a League Cup, European Cup Winners' Cup and European Super Cup. Edwards said: "I believe we have got the best possible manager for the job. Our meeting to decide who we wanted came out with a unanimous decision for Alex Ferguson. The new manager will be under the same ruling as Ron Atkinson when it comes to any further spending. We have a big staff of 20 players, which is already too many. He will have to sell before he can buy, the same as Ron Atkinson was told."

Back in Aberdeen the media frenzy surrounded the next step for Aberdeen. Archie Knox had turned down the chance to stay on as manager in his own right, choosing to follow his friend to England, and two names dominated the headlines as the hunt for Ferguson's successor began: Sandy Jardine and Willie Miller.

Miller was an obvious candidate, even though he still had several seasons as a player in front of him, while Jardine, assistant to Alex MacDonald at Hearts, was the departing manager's own recommendation to the Aberdeen board. When Ian Porterfield was revealed as the choice it came as a bolt from the blue, it was an appointment nobody had predicted.

While Porterfield struggled to fill the gap left by his illustrious predecessor and the 1986/87 campaign ended without silverware, Ferguson also toiled initially as he attempted to rebuild a crumbling giant of the English game. The well documented dark days, when he was within a whisker of being dismissed by the Old Trafford side, were soon banished to the history books as the plan fell into place and a familiar trophy trail began.

It started with the FA Cup win in 1990, followed by the European Cup Winners' Cup in 1991 as he became the first manager to win the trophy with two different clubs. The League Cup was claimed the following year and in 1993 a 26 year wait for the league championship ended. Ferguson, a hero to the Aberdeen fans, was elevated to the same status at Manchester United.

He told the jubilant Red Devils faithful: "This can be just the start for Manchester United. We have the platform, we have the resources and we definitely have the players. Now it's up to them and how hungry they are. The door is open for us. The future looks good at the moment but I won't be taking my foot off the pedal – that's not in my nature."

He stayed true to his word and the success has not dried up. All in all, up to the end of the 2006/07 season, the godfather of Scottish management can lay claim to nine league titles, the FA Cup five times, two wins in the League Cup, the European Cup Winners' Cup and the European Super Cup in 1991 and the holy grail of the European Cup in 1999. For a man who was unemployed when he initially landed on the doorstep at Pittodrie, it is a remarkable list of achievements.

the mix remains the same just as it did during his Pittodrie adventure, with a strong reliance in giving young players their chance

Ferguson celebrated his 21st anniversary as Manchester United manager in 2007 and he now finds himself closing in on Sir Matt Busby's record of 24 years at the helm. Now past his 65th birthday, the driving ambition which made him stand out at Aberdeen is still every bit as evident.

Ferguson celebrated his 21st year in charge by booming: "The players clearly want to do well in the Champions League and if you are one of the best, you naturally look to spell it out with cups and medals. Otherwise you are in danger of ending your career as a nearly man – and I don't think a single Manchester United player wants that. I sense that the mood is good and the commitment is there for a really determined effort this season to put our club firmly back on the European map. Talk comes cheap, I know, but we have built a platform that, with just a little bit of luck, will launch us on our way to capture this most elusive of trophies. There has always been great ability in our teams but this one - since I took stock and brought in a new element - is maturing fast and I am convinced the players are ready to deliver."

Just as he had predicted European glory when he started the journey with the Dons, Ferguson has confidence in the squad of superstars he has assembled. Money is not an object, retaining players is no concern – yet Ferguson remains ruthless in his pursuit of success. Of the squad which won the European Cup in 1999 only Gary Neville, Paul Scholes, Ryan Giggs and Wes Brown remain on the staff.

Whether he passes Busby's amazing service record is a matter for Ferguson to decide but he insists he is more concerned with the trophy count than the number of years next to his name.

He added: "There's obviously an impact from Sir Matt Busby's reign. I think back to what he actually started after the war and had the vision to take Manchester United into Europe in 1956. He was before his time. So that's the real link I have with him, the years I've spent here have been about achieving, about entertaining."

In his early days, making a name for himself as a young emerging manager, Ferguson's team at St Mirren was renowned throughout the land as a carefree group who were tasked with thrilling the Love Street faithful. The hair is grey, the face has aged and the stage is far bigger but the philosophy has remained untouched in the years that have followed. In fact, the methods have altered little despite the added sophistication that decades of experience have added to the package. The mix remains just the same as it did during his Pittodrie adventure, with a strong reliance on giving young players their chance when it is merited and marrying those home-grown products with cleverly recruited signings. The budget has changed beyond all recognition, Ferguson shops in Harrods rather than Tesco nowadays, but the process remains much the same and the quest for perfection just as strong.

QUARTER-FINAL SECOND LEG, ABERDEEN v BAYERN MUNICH
MARCH 16, 1983: ABERDEEN 3, BAYERN MUNICH 2

E**VEN** before the first leg on the continent had been played the Pittodrie encounter had sold out, ensuring an electric atmosphere for the biggest night in the club's history.

Ferguson was confident in the hours before the second leg showdown in the north-east, predicting: "You can take it as read that Bayern will be far more positive at Pittodrie. They know they have got to do something this time, but we are well prepared for the match and we know we can beat the best German football has to offer in our own ground. We defeated Hamburg last season at Pittodrie and I know we have a chance of winning again."

The Germans were rattled and pushed a £1,250 per man bonus on the table for victory at Pittodrie. Trailing Hamburg in the Bundesliga and out of the national cup competition, the European Cup Winners' Cup was last chance saloon for Bayern.

Ferguson said: "We must play with patience but it would be nice to introduce a flavour of Scottish-type football as well. The younger members of the team reacted magnificently in conquering tension in the first leg and now they can go out and play their own game, while remembering that it is a European tie. I have told them that there is no need for them to be afraid of the occasion."

There was one change for the draw in the first leg, with Doug Bell dropping to the bench to accommodate Gordon Strachan following his return to full fitness.

Bayern's coach Pal Csernai, a Hungarian who had played his football in Austria and Germany, countered Strachan's inclusion by calling up Wolfgang Dremmler to go head to head with the Scotland international.

It was Ferguson who triumphed in the tactical chess game, his check-mate moment coming with the introduction of match winning hero John Hewitt from the bench in the pulsating 3-2 second round win to book the coveted semi-final place. The adventure continued and no script writer could have come up with a more dramatic way to do it.

● Gordon Strachan's young fan club in the stand at Pittodrie before the Bayern Munich home leg.

ABERDEEN STRIKE BACK

ABERDEEN	3
BAYERN MUNICH	2

(Aggregate 3-2)

● Eric Black heads the ball past Bayern goalkeeper Muller for Neil Simpson to make it 1-1

● *By Alastair Macdonald*

ABERDEEN created a piece of club history at Pittodrie last night when they scored a dramatic victory over triple European Cup winners Bayern Munich – and a glorious page was written in what must undoubtedly be the most fantastic European tie ever seen at the Aberdeen ground.

Twice in arrears in this crunch European Cup Winners' Cup quarter-final second leg, the Dons rose magnificently to the challenge and equalised on each occasion before finally taking the lead for the firt time in the tie in the 77th minute.

When Aberdeen lost a goal in the 10th minute – only the second goal they had conceded in 640 minutes of European football this season – the outlook looked bleak for the Pittodrie side.

Retaining the discipline and composure which have marked so many of their displays this season the Aberdeen side equalised through Neil Simpson before the interval.

Bayern, looking much more like a team of their reputation than they had in the first leg, snatched a surprise lead early in the second half but even this failed to dim the Dons spirits and they produced two goals within the space of a minute.

Alex McLeish headed the second equaliser and then John Hewitt, a substitute for Simpson only two minutes earlier, maintained his reputation for scoring in European events by snatching the winner.

When the final whistle sounded with the Dons well in control the Aberdeen players were immediately swamped by their jubilant fans and the Aberdeen team paid their own tribute to the support they received by coming out onto the pitch again a few minutes later.

As in the goalless first leg in Munich the Dons performance was once again a triumph of teamwork with all 13 players on view making their contribution.

TO MASTER MUNICH

● Alex McLeish and Willie Miller look on during some more frantic penalty box action.

GERMANS SUNK BY SUPER-SUB HEWITT

ABERDEEN opened with a lightning raid on the right but McGhee's determined attempt to retain possession brought a free kick for Bayern.

Rougvie and Cooper were each spoken to by the French referee within the first two minutes for the fierceness of their tackling.

A momentary hesitation by Dremmler in the Bayern penalty box saw Weir rob him, but the Aberdeen winger could not get in a shot.

Aberdeen's early pressure forced three corners in the opening five minutes and the goalmouth resembled a sardine can as Weir took the flag kicks.

Simpson got in a shot in nine minutes after McGhee had side-footed a Weir cross into his path.

Bayern were under pressure, but they relieved it in the most effective way by taking the lead in 10 minutes.

It was a disputed free kick following a Hoeness-McLeish clash 30 yards from goal which cost Aberdeen dearly.

Breitner side-footed the free kick to AUGENTHALER who moved

● John Hewitt forces home the winner to clinch a dramatic 3-2 victory

to the edge of the box, veered away from a Black challenge and sent a right foot shot at Leighton who got a hand to the ball but could not keep it out of the net.

Aberdeen responded spiritedly but apart from a promising run by Strachan, which finally faded out, the German rearguard was not seriously troubled.

Bayern created another dangerous opening in 17 minutes when Rummenigge sent Del'Haye away on his own on the right. Leighton, however, left his line to fend off the Bayern raider's try.

Aberdeen supporters were cheered by a near-miss in 22 minutes. Kennedy, taking a short

corner from Weir, curled over a tempting ball but Black's header rebounded from the face of the crossbar and the resultant mele ended with Simpson firing ove the bar.

The pace was fast and furious with both goals under threat fo spells.

The German goal was lucky t survive in 34 minutes whe Muller dived to cut out a Wei cross from the right and minute later Cooper had a sh deflected by a defender's body.

The Dons pressure, however, wi rewarded with an equalisir goal in 38 minutes. A beautiful judged cross from McGh evaded Muller's leap and four

...ack just beyond the far post. ...though Augenthaler blocked ...ack's header on the line ...MPSON, following up, forced ...e ball into the net despite the ...orts of the German defender to ...ve a second time.

...is was the spark of ...couragement the Dons needed ...d the German goal underwent ...steady barrage in the closing ...inutes of the half, Aberdeen ...ming close to taking the lead in ... minutes when Augenthaler ...ain came to his side's rescue by ...ocking the ball on line.

...remmler halted a McGhee raid ... the expense of a free kick just ...tside the German box in the ...cond minute of the second half ...d Simpson tested Muller with a ...erce grounder from Strachan's ...de-footed free kick.

... solo break from Rummenigge ...oked dangerous for Aberdeen ...vo minutes later but Bayern's ...ading marksman did not make ...e most of his opportunity and ...as dispossessed before getting in ... shot.

...s in the first leg Del'Haye's pace ...n the right wing was giving the ...berdeen defence most trouble ...ut his crosses were being ...opped up in the middle.

... Strachan burst through the ...niddle in 58 minutes brought the ...ons a free kick but Weir's ...ttempt to score direct from 20 ...ards saw the ball go over the bar.

...ragedy for the Dons when

Bayern scored a goal out of the blue in 61 minutes. Del'Haye and Dremmler combined on the right and the full back's high cross was back headed by Hoeness to PFLUGLER. The reserve defender's swerving left-foot shot beat Leighton at the foot of the near post.

Five minutes later Aberdeen substituted McMaster for Kennedy.

Rougvie switched to right back with Cooper at left back and the newcomer in midfield.

Muller required treatment after clashing with McLeish at a corner kick in 69 minutes. But the German keeper recovered sufficiently to pull off a brilliant reflex save two minutes later when Black got his head to a Weir cross only yards from the line.

Aberdeen introduced their second substitute in 75 minutes when Hewitt replaced Simpson and the change produced almost immediate dividends with the Dons scoring twice within the space of a minute to take the lead for the first time in the overall tie.

In 76 minutes Strachan and McMaster fooled the German defence with their "dummy" free kick routine. After the two Aberdeen players appeared to get in each other's way at the first attempt Strachan quickly wheeled and lobbed the free kick into the goalmouth where

McLEISH was waiting to find the net with a strong header.

The excitement among the Dons fans had no time to subside before the Dons scored again. Muller produced another brilliant save from a close range Black header but the ball bounced clear for HEWITT to launch himself at it and volley it into the net.

The shocked Germans made an effort to retrieve the situation with an 83rd minute substitution when Mathy replaced Pflugler but the Dons were in command of the situation.

As in Munich, Aberdeen finished the game playing pattern football, retaining possession.

Hewitt went down under a heavy tackle in the final minute but recovered in time to hear the final whistle and be engulfed along with his team-mates as hundreds of young Dons fans rushed onto the pitch.

ABERDEEN – Leighton, Kennedy (McMaster), Rougvie, Cooper, McLeish, Miller, Strachan, Simpson (Hewitt), McGhee, Black, Weir.

BAYERN MUNICH – Miller, Dremmler, Horsmann, Grobe, Augenthaler, Kraus, Pflugler (Mathy), Breitner, Hoeness, Del Haye, Rummenigge.

Referee: M. Vautrot (France).

● Neil Simpson watches his goal hit the Bayern net (top) just before being grounded by a German defender (bottom).

Muller collects the ball ahead of Mark cGhee (top) while Gordon Strachan puts essure on the Munich defence (bottom).

● The jubilant Aberdeen players take their bow in front of the Dons supportes at full time while John Hewitt (top inset) and Neale Cooper (bottom inset) accept the congratulations of the supporters

● Skipper Willie Miller is mobbed by ecstatic supporters (top), the Pittodrie dressing room scenes post match (middle) and John Hewitt, Alex McLeish and Neil Simpson toast the team's success (bottom).

jim leighton

Born: 24 July 1958, Johnstone

Aberdeen appearances: League 382, Scottish Cup 49, League Cup 54, Europe 43

First Dons game: League, 12 August 1978 v Hearts (a) won 4-1

Pittodrie honours: Premier Division (1984, 1985), Scottish Cup (1982, 1983 1984, 1986), League Cup (1985), European Cup Winners' Cup (1983), European Super Cup (1983),

Other teams: Scotland (91 caps), Manchester United, Dundee, Hibs

Did you know? Prior to playing for Aberdeen, Jim Leighton served as a civil servant in the unemployment benefit office at Kinning Park in Rangers territory in Glasgow. His role was to work with homeless claimants and his mixed bag of clients included a doctor, a boxer, a dentist and a one legged man who had a habit of losing his wooden limb on his journeys to the office. The goalkeeper, who once quit football for a year as a youngster after being dropped, combined his profession with his blossoming career in junior football and planned to continue his double life until the Dons made him a full-time offer he simply could not refuse and he turned his back on the civil service to concentrate on making a name for himself in professional sport.

ABERDEEN FC

1

ABERDEEN FOOTBALL CLUB

doug rougvie

Born: 24 May 1956, Ballingry

Aberdeen appearances: League 181+19, Scottish Cup 26, League Cup 45+7, Europe 28+2

Goals: League 19, League Cup 2

First Dons game: League Cup, 9 August 1975 v Celtic (a) lost 1-0.

Honours: Premier Division (1980, 1984), Scottish Cup (1982, 1983, 1984). European Cup Winners' Cup (1983), European Super Cup (1983).

Other teams: Scotland (1 cap), Keith, Chelsea, Brighton, Shrewsbury, Fulham, Dunfermline, Montrose (manager), Huntly (manager), Cove Rangers (manager).

Did you know? Doug Rougvie can claim to have a common bond with David Beckham. The rugged Fifer may be a million miles from the pampered former England captain but both have been the target of a flying boot launched by Sir Alex Ferguson. While Beckham's high profile injury as the result of Fergie's fury at Manchester United became headline news instantly, Rougvie's brush with the gaffer behind closed doors was kept under wraps for more than two decades. The big defender managed to duck out of the way when the boots flew in the Pittodrie dressing room and his manager never forgot, with Ferguson making reference to the incident in his recent biography as he explained his part in the Beckham saga and the emotions he has always displayed as a manager. Sandwiches were Ferguson's other weapon of choice during his frequent outbursts in front of Rougvie and the rest of the Dons squad.

ABERDEEN FC 2

ABERDEEN FOOTBALL CLUB

john mcmaster

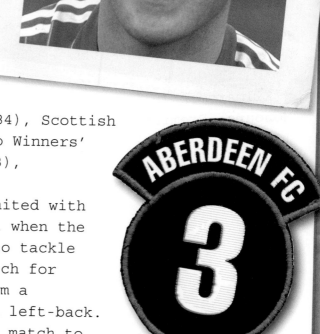

Born: 23 February 1955, Greenock.
Aberdeen appearances: League 205+32, Scottish Cup 29+5, League Cup 54+7, Europe 28+3.
Goals: League 20, Scottish Cup 4, League Cup 9
First Dons game: League Cup, 24 August 1974 v Dunfermline (h) won 3-0
Honours: Premier Division (1980, 1984), Scottish Cup (1982, 1983. 1986), European Cup Winners' Cup (1983), European Super Cup (1983),
Other teams: Peterhead, Morton
Did you know? John McMaster was reunited with former Aberdeen mentor Billy McNeill when the Celtic legend picked a select side to tackle the Dons in the 1985 testimonial match for McMaster, who had been converted from a midfielder to become an accomplished left-back. A crowd of 16,500 turned out for the match to show their appreciation for a player who had overcome serious injury to keep his Aberdeen career alive and they were treated to a game featuring the likes of Liverpool manager Kenny Dalglish. McMaster had been told he would never play again by surgeons who operated on him just hours after he had been cut down in full flow by Liverpool defender Ray Kennedy during a 1980 European Cup tie on Merseyside but he defied medical opinion to come back even stronger than before.

ABERDEEN FC 3

neale cooper

Born: 24 November 1963, Darjeeling.

Aberdeen appearances: League 133+16, Scottish Cup 27+2, League Cup 27+1, Europe 33+6

Goals: League 6, Scottish Cup 3, League Cup 1

First Dons game: 11 October 1980 v Kilmarnock (h) won 2-0

Honours: Premier Division (1984, 1985), Scottish Cup (1982, 1983, 1984, 1986), League Cup (1985), European Cup Winners' Cup (1983), European Super Cup (1983),

Other teams: Aston Villa, Rangers, Reading, Dunfermline, Ross County (manager), Hartlepool (manager), Gillingham (manager), Peterhead (manager).

Did you know? Neale Cooper was the only player in the Gothenburg team born outside of the British isles. Despite being Scottish through and through, the midfielder was born in India after his parents had emigrated to work in the tea planting industry. He returned to the north-east as a youngster and progressed through school and juvenile football in Aberdeen, his home city despite his more exotic birthplace. Cooper could yet have a part to play in Scotland's football future as his son, Alex, begins to climb the international ladder. The teenager, signed by Liverpool from Ross County in 2008, is a Scotland youth cap and is being tipped to follow in his father's footsteps and make it to the very top.

ABERDEEN FC

4

alex mcleish

Born: 21 January 1959, Barrhead
Aberdeen appearances: League 493+2, Scottish Cup 68+3, League Cup 74+1, Europe 56+1
Goals: League 25, Scottish Cup 2, League Cup 2, Europe 1
Honours: Premier Division (1980, 1984, 1985), Scottish Cup (1982, 1983, 1984, 1986, 1990), League Cup (1985, 1989), European Cup Winners' Cup (1983), European Super Cup (1983).
First Dons game: League, 2 January 1978 v Dundee United (h) won 1-0
Other teams: Scotland (77 caps plus manager), Motherwell (manager), Hibs (manager), Rangers (manager) Birmingham City (manager)

Did you know? Alex McLeish played in front of Jim Leighton well before the duo helped form the backbone upon which the Gothenburg success was built. He and the Dons goalkeeping legend Jim Leighton were team-mates as youngsters at Glasgow United and traveled together to Aberdeen for trials at Pittodrie as they embarked on the fantastic journey which brought so much success. The juvenile team responsible for two Gothenburg greats folded in 1988, two years before youth product McLeish was crowned player of the year by the Scottish Football Writers' Association. Leighton was not the only link to the past for McLeish at the Ullevi Stadium when he lined up against Real Madrid in 1983 - winger Peter Weir attended the same school, Barrhead High.

ABERDEEN FC

5

Born: 2 May 1955, Glasgow

Aberdeen appearances: League 560+1, Scottish Cup 66, League Cup 109, Europe 61

Goals: League 19, Scottish Cup 6, League Cup 3, Europe 2

Honours: Premier Division (1980, 1984, 1985), Scottish Cup (1982, 1983, 1984,1986), League Cup (1976, 1985, 1989), European Cup Winners' Cup (1983), European Super Cup (1983).

First Dons game: 28 April 1973 v Morton (a) won 2-1

Manager: February 1992-February 1995

Other teams: Scotland (65 caps)

Did you know? Willie Miller was appointed captain at Pittodrie on the recommendation of the man he replaced. Goalkeeper Bobby Clark handed over responsibility to the 20 year-old in December 1975 having pinpointed Miller as the ideal man to take on the role. Manager Ally MacLeod agreed and, after a two game spell as acting skipper, the defender took on the extra duties permanently. Clark had been a reluctant captain, claiming the job was better suited to an outfield player. Miller claimed at the time that he had been quiet since his introduction to the first team but vowed to change and he grew into the role in style, becoming famed for his influence over his team-mates and referees.

ABERDEEN FOOTBALL CLUB

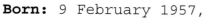

gordon strachan

Born: 9 February 1957, Edinburgh

Aberdeen appearances: League 183+8, Scottish Cup 29, League Cup 46+3, Europe 34+4

Goals: League 54, Scottish Cup 7, League Cup 20, Europe 8

Honours: Premier Division (1980, 1984), Scottish Cup (1982, 1983, 1984), European Cup Winners Cup (1983), European Super Cup (1983).

First Dons game: 5 November 1977 v Dundee United (a) won 1-0

Other teams: Scotland (50 caps), Dundee, Manchester United, Leeds United, Coventry City (player and manager), Southampton United (manager), Celtic (manager).

Did you know? Gordon Strachan rejected an approach from Manchester United when he was a 14 year-old schoolboy. The Edinburgh youngster had already agreed to join Dundee when the Old Trafford giants made their move and Strachan refused to go back on his word and went straight from school to the Dens Park staff. It took him 13 years to finally wind his way to United, who were forced to pay big money to land a player they had tried to pick up for nothing.

neil simpson

Born: 15 November 1961, London

Aberdeen appearances: League 200+19, Scottish Cup 34, League Cup 33+4, Europe 37+5

Goals: League 19, Scottish Cup 5, League Cup 1, Europe 6.

Honours: Premier Division (1984, 1985), Scottish Cup (1982, 1983, 1984), League Cup (1985), European Cup Winners' Cup (1983), European Super Cup (1983).

First Dons game: League, 20 December 1980 v Partick Thistle (a) drew 1-1

Also played for: Scotland (5 caps), Newcastle United, Motherwell, Cove Rangers.

Did you know? Neil Simpson's commitment to grass roots football began long before he was appointed assistant director to Aberdeen's recently launched youth academy. In his early 20s as a player at Pittodrie he spent time coaching the team at his old primary school in Newmachar and helped the youngsters to cup success. He would cheer on the children's team from the touchline on Saturday mornings and also would often dash away from home games for the Dons to watch the Newmachar school team play in tournaments in the city in the late afternoon. A decade later Simpson, having retired from playing, was appointed by the SFA as the north's first ever independent football development officer as his passion for promoting young talent continued, leading to his return to the Dons in a community role and subsequently his position within the new academy structure.

ABERDEEN FC

8

ABERDEEN FOOTBALL CLUB

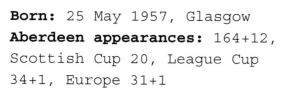

Born: 25 May 1957, Glasgow

Aberdeen appearances: 164+12, Scottish Cup 20, League Cup 34+1, Europe 31+1

Goals: League 61, Scottish Cup 7, League Cup 18, Europe 14

Honours: Premier Division (1980, 1984), Scottish Cup (1982, 1983, 1984), European Cup Winners Cup (1983), European Super Cup (1983).

First Dons game: 1 April 1979 v Morton (a) won 1-0

Also played for: Scotland (4 caps), Morton, Newcastle, SV Hamburg, Celtic, Reading (manager), Leicester City (manager), Wolverhampton Wanderers (manager), Millwall (manager), Brighton (manager), Motherwell (manager).

Did you know? Mark McGhee became only the second British player to turn out for Hamburg when he followed in the illustrious footsteps of Kevin Keegan, who was on the books from 1977 to 1980. The deal which took him to Germany was reported to have been worth in excess of £80,000 per year to the departing Dons star and the lucrative contract also included a club Mercedes as well as a house provided by Hamburg to fit his new superstar lifestyle. The continental side invested in a three-year contract to secure the services of a player who had scored against them in the European Super Cup final and had to pay £300,000 compensation to Aberdeen.

ABERDEEN FOOTBALL CLUB

eric black

Born: 1 October 1963, Bellshill
Aberdeen appearances: League 115+19, Scottish Cup 25+3, League Cup 18+4, Europe 22+4
Goals: League 45, Scottish Cup 5, League Cup 12, Europe 7
Honours: Premier Division (1984), Scottish Cup (1982, 1983, 1984), League Cup(1985), European Cup Winners Cup (1983), European Super Cup (1983).
First Dons game: League, 31 October 1981 v Dundee United (h) draw 1-1
Other teams: Scotland (2 caps), Metz, Celtic (coach), Motherwell (manager), Coventry City (manager), Birmingham City (coach), Wigan (coach)

Did you know? The back injury which forced Eric Black's retirement from football in 1990, at the age of 27, could be traced back to his Aberdeen days. He fell awkwardly while playing for the Dons against Motherwell at Fir Park on September 10 1983 and suffered intermittent problems from then on. By the time he eventually called time on his playing career he was sent to Luxemburg by Metz for treatment designed to prevent disability in the future, with fears about crippling arthritis developing. Black had played for the French side by using painkilling injections, with his final appearance lasting 15 minutes when he came on from the bench to face Nancy. Further examinations revealed two stress fractures in the lower back which were thought to date back more than five years and, explaining the agony he had endured over a prolonged period.

ABERDEEN FC
10

ABERDEEN FOOTBALL CLUB

peter weir

Born: 18 January 1958, Johnstone

Aberdeen appearances: League 160+11, Scottish Cup 19+2, League Cup 28+1, Europe 29+3

Goals: League 23, Scottish Cup 7, League Cup 2, Europe 6

Honours: Premier Division (1984, 1985), Scottish Cup (1983, 1984, 1986), European Cup Winners' Cup (1983), European Super Cup (1983).

First Dons game: League Cup, 8 August 1981 v Kilmarnock (h) won 3-0

Other teams: Scotland (6 caps), St Mirren, Leicester City, Ayr United

Did you know? Aberdeen were almost responsible for Peter Weir turning his back on playing the game which made him a star. Weir stopped playing at the age of 15 to concentrate on following Aberdeen home and away as a supporter – from his family home in Glasgow. Weir's love affair with the Dons stemmed from the 1970 Scottish Cup final, which he attended with his father as a neutral and ended up in the Aberdeen end. The Pittodrie side won 3-1 and Weir was hooked, despite the fact he had no link to the north-east apart from a distant relative in Forfar. During his days as a Dons follower he worked as an assistant green keeper but returned to playing amateur football at the age of 19 before progressing to Neilston juniors and the senior game under Alex Ferguson at St Mirren.

john hewitt

Born: 9 February 1963, Aberdeen

Aberdeen apearances: League 201+65, Scottish Cup 30+10, League Cup 41+11, Europe 41+14

Goals: League 52, Scottish Cup 8, League Cup 13, Europe 12

Honours: Premier Division (1984, 1985), Scottish Cup (1982, 1983, 1986), League Cup (1985), European Cup Winners' Cup (1983), European Super Cup (1983).

First Dons game: League, 15 December 1979 v St Mirren (h) won 2-0

Other teams: Celtic, Middlesborough, St Mirren, Ross County, Cove Rangers, Dundalk (manager).

Did you know? John Hewitt's name will be set in stone at Aberdeen's home ground regardless of what happens to his old Pittodrie stomping ground in the future. Hewitt was chosen as the man to lay the first sett at the Centenary Way outside of the current Richard Donald Stand as part of the club's 100th birthday celebrations. It was agreed that the commemorative stones, each inscribed with a message, will be carefully moved if the club eventually gets its wish of a new stadium elsewhere in the city. Hewitt's stone is inscribed simply with: "I scored it".

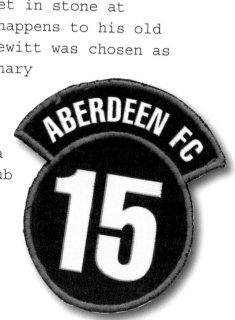

WHERE ARE THEY NOW?

**HE** net does not have to be cast far or wide to land a Gothenburg great. Jim Leighton, Willie Miller, Neil Simpson, John McMaster and Peter Weir are all back on the Pittodrie payroll in varying roles to provide a permanent link to the glory days of the past.

In one shape or form all five are tasked with bringing the good times back to the famous old ground by unearthing and then grooming the next generation of home grown Dons players, just as Alex Ferguson and his scouting and coaching team did all those years ago.

In his role as director of football Miller is the figurehead and the guiding light for a youth network under constant revision and development as the club strives to rediscover the golden touch. Leighton, serving as the goalkeeping coach to the senior team as well as the reserves and youth sides, and scout McMaster maintain the Gothenburg link to the first team. The remaining two are back at grass roots level in key roles.

Simpson and Weir are both assistant directors at the club's youth academy, launched in 2006 despite the lack of a permanent training base. Simpson is passing on his expertise and experience to the north-east's promising young players, concentrating on the under-10 to under-13 age bracket, while Weir is based in Glasgow and tasked with heading a team of five coaches in the south.

Weir is relishing his role and believes the bid to regain ground in the race to get to Scotland's best emerging players. He said: "I've been an Aberdeen supporter since I was a boy. It started when my dad got tickets for the 1970 cup final, when Celtic were beaten 3-1, and we stood in the Dons end. After that I started travelling to games on the supporters' bus and on the train right through the 1970s. To be back working with the club now is fantastic, it's crazy how these things work out.

"We're beginning to make good headway with attracting good young players to the club. None of the boys we have approached have turned us down, quite the opposite – we have recently had one turning down a good offer from Rangers to join us instead.

"Rangers and Celtic are trying to nip in and sign many of the same players and there are scouts from so many other clubs watching them too. What we try to do is treat the kids right and treat the parents right and demonstrate that they have a chance to progress with Aberdeen."

Weir believes the legacy of those glory days can help him recruit the next generation of Pittodrie stars. He added: "Of course we can't say Aberdeen will win a European trophy again but we also can't believe it is impossible. The Gothenburg team was packed full of young players who had come through the ranks at the club and formed a tremendous team and we are striving to return to the days when the club was producing so many quality players."

Weir's route back to Pittodrie was a winding one. After leaving for Leicester City in 1988 he ended up back in Scotland with St Mirren less than 12 months later. In 1990 he moved south to continue his playing career with Ayr United before retiring at the age of 34 due to an ankle injury.

He first moved into scouting under Tommy Burns, both at Kilmarnock and Celtic, before branching out into coaching as assistant to former Dons team-mate Billy Stark at Morton in the late 1990s. Rangers spotted his potential and enlisted him to help with the Ibrox youth development programme before Miller tempted him back to Aberdeen in 2006.

Simpson arrived back on the club's staff initially working in the Dons community department having cut his teeth in a similar Elgin-based role with the Scottish Football Association.

Having moved to England with Newcastle in 1990, Simpson returned north to join Motherwell a year later. Two seasons at Fir Park were followed by a brief cameo with Cove Rangers in his native north-east before injury brought the curtain down on his playing career.

His time with Aberdeen was by far the most profitable and it is that period in the former Scotland cap's career that lends the greatest inspiration in his coaching career.

Simpson said: "We used to come in and train on the Pittodrie car park but the quality of training with Bobby Clark and Lenny Taylor was first class. More than anything they tought us so much about the commitment and work ethic that every player needs. If you look at the best players in the world, they haven't got where they are with talent alone - they all have the desire to be the best and the right attitude.

"I've been through the system myself and we want to recreate a modern equivalent of what the club had then, when so many good young players were coming through. In the Gothenburg team alone Jim Leighton, Doug Rougvie, Alex McLeish, Willie Miller, Neale Cooper, Eric Black, John Hewitt and I had all joined as kids hoping to make the grade."

Simpson concedes the game has changed since the glory days of the 1980s and not all of the developments have been positive.

He added: "Where it is different now is that we have to show kids some of the basic skills that people used to pick up in the playground or playing on the streets. There has to be an emphasis on coaching to compensate for fact kids are spending less time playing in those environments but at the same time we have to strike a balance of allowing young players to express themselves and develop the ability to do things off the cuff.

"I never played organised football at primary school, with maybe the exception of one game for the school at Newmachar, and everything I did was small sided with friends in the park or playground. Now our kids are involved in organised teams from an earlier age and we have to make sure they can thrive in that environment.

"I really enjoy what I'm doing. It may be three of four years until the players in my age group are at the stage of turning full-time so there's a long term goal to aim for. I want to see as many of them coming through and giving Neil Cooper the best young players in the country for the under-19 team."

Dundee threw Leighton a lifeline in 1992 in a £200,000 deal and he won a first division medal

Leighton is another of the vital cogs in the current Dons machine, with a succession of goalkeepers benefiting from his vast experience at the very top of the game. He notched up 91 international appearances before retiring in 1998 and remains the most capped shot stopper in Scotland's history.

He benefits from the experience of three World Cup finals - in Mexico in 1986, Italy four years later and France in 1998 – and a mixed club career. His dream move to Manchester United turned sour in 1990 when he was dropped for the FA Cup final replay against Crystal Palace, after being held up as a scapegoat for the shock 3-3 result in the first final. Dundee threw Leighton a lifeline in 1992 in a £200,000 deal and he won a First Division medal before moving on to Hibs in 1993, leading to a Scotland recall the following year. He made close to 200 appearances for the East Road side before his Aberdeen homecoming in 1997 for a three year stint which was brought to an end by a facial injury in the 2000 Scottish Cup final against Rangers at the age of 41. It was his 531st game for the Dons but not the end of his special relationship with the club, who retained his services as a specialist coach.

McMaster also continues to have an input in first team affairs at Pittodrie, compiling reports on opposition teams for Jimmy Calderwood as well as scouting for fresh talent in the Glasgow area as part of Weir's team in the south.

After leaving Aberdeen during Ian Porterfield's reign, McMaster returned to his hometown club Morton as player-coach and went on to serve as assistant manager. Despite his link to the Cappielow side, McMaster's loyalty will always be with Aberdeen and that passion was reciprocated by the Dons fans when 16,500 turned out for his testimonial match against a Billy McNeill Select in 1985. He overcame a serious knee injury suffered in the 1980 European Cup tie against Liverpool to play his part in the 1983 European triumph.

While Leighton, Simpson and Weir are at the coal face working with the gems the recently introduced academy system is designed to polish, several of their Gothenburg colleagues are in a position to take advantage of those efforts beneath the surface.

Alex McLeish is, of course the highest profile of all. While defensive partner Miller's brush with frontline management proved unrewarding, the flame haired Dons talisman quickly emerged as one of the country's most promising coaching talents after making the leap into that side of the game with Motherwell in 1994 and steering his new team to second place in his first season in charge.

His steady climb up the ladder continued with his move to Hibs in 1998, guiding the Leith club to the First Division title in 1999 after the pain of relegation the previous term. His progress in Edinburgh began to draw attention and in 2001 Rangers tempted McLeish to Ibrox where he won championships in 2003 and 2005 as well as the Scottish Cup twice and the League Cup three times. He also became the first manager to lead a Scottish team into the last 16 of the Champions League.

When he was replaced by Paul Le Guen in 2006 the Dons legend faced a crossroads in his coaching career. Walter Smith's decision to quit as Scotland manager to replace Le Guen early in 2007 provided new direction, with McLeish the overwhelming favourite to pick up the baton.

It was a hard act to follow but McLeish did it in style, most notably leading his country to victory against the mighty France in Paris in September 2007 during the incredible Euro 2008 qualifying campaign which saw the national team left requiring victory in the final game against world champions Italy to make it through. It proved a bridge too far, but the effort was admirable even if the objective was unachievable.

The 1-0 success against the French, courtesy of James McFadden's wonder goal, was in fact made in Aberdeen. Pre-match, McLeish harked back to his days as a Dons player to inspire his Scotland charges. Standing in the Parc des Princes he said: "This is the place to be. Whenever I used to go into these grounds in the days of Archie Knox and Alex Ferguson with Aberdeen, Archie's line was always 'if you can't play football in an arena like this ...' and it always gave you a bit of a buzz. Those words have always stuck in my head. Every time you play in places like these it enhances your education and it is a privilege – you are doing something millions of other people will never get the chance to savour

Gordon Strachan is of course the other headline grabbing Gothenburg great making it big in Scottish managment

or experience. The ground that made biggest impression made on me was Bayern Munich's Olympic Stadium – at the time it was something spectacular."

McLeish called time on his Scotland tenure late in 2007 when his desire to get back to the hands on life of club management proved too strong and the challenge of Birmingham City tempted him to the promised land of the Premiership.

Gordon Strachan is of course the other headline grabbing Gothenburg great making it big in Scottish management, a former Old Firm foe of McLeish when he landed the Celtic manager's job in 2005 when he succeeded Martin O'Neill.

It was Strachan's first venture back in the Scottish top flight since his Dons days. When Manchester United decided to sell him in 1989 it was Leeds United who met the £200,000 asking price and installed the diminutive midfielder as captain as the Elland Road side marched to the Second Division title before the dream Premiership title success in 1992.

Coventry was the final stop on Strachan's playing adventure and the first port of call on his managerial journey. He took charge of the Midlands club in 1996 and spent five years at the helm before a three year stint with Southampton and his eventual return home with Celtic, where he brought the title home at the first attempt and successfully defended it in 2006/07.

Former Dons team-mate Mark McGhee is one of the managers aiming to put a spoke in Strachan's wheel at Parkhead. McGhee is another Gothenburg hero reacquainting himself with Scottish football after a considerable absence.

The leading scorer in the European run of 1983 found himself back in his home country in the summer of 2007 when he accepted the top job at Motherwell, replacing Maurice Malpas after the club had endured a miserable 2006/07 season. McGhee's impact was immediate as Well stormed back up the SPL table and the relegation fears of the previous season faded into the past.

When McGhee left Pittodrie in 1985 he had dreams of continental stardom with SV Hamburg but injury tempered that ambition and it was with Celtic, between 1986 and 1989, that he rediscovered his form and fitness. He first moved to England with Newcastle post-Celtic and got his managerial break with Reading in 1991.

His reputation soon grew and stints with Leicester, Wolves, Millwall and Brighton followed for a man very much in demand. McGhee took charge of Reading when their current Premiership status was not even a distant dream. The club languished in the old Third Division, competing alongside the likes of Torquay and Exeter, but the rookie coach was determined to learn the ropes the hard way. Just as Sir Alex Ferguson had done all those years ago with East Stirling. Progress was steady until 1994 when McGhee led Reading to the League One championship title, pipping Port Vale by a single point.

He helped the club gain a foothold in the Championship the following term but within four months Leicester City lured him to the Midlands. He spent 51 weeks with the Foxes, drafted in to try and preserve their Premiership status but unable to keep them in the top flight.

In the final weeks of 1995 McGhee was poached by Wolves. His best finish during his three year stint at Molineux was third in the 1996/97 campaign as the sleeping giant of English football refused to be wakened from its slumber under its Scottish leader.

Three years with Millwall, between September 2000 and the tail end of 2003, brought the League One championship in 2001 and with Brighton, where he spent a further three years, the champagne kept flowing as the Seagulls enjoyed promotion to the Championship through the play-offs in 2004.

Neale Cooper is another of Sir Alex's proteges to have carved out a management career on both sides of the border. After two years at Aston Villa following his departure from Pittodrie, playing under Graham Taylor and Billy McNeill, Cooper moved back to Scotland as part of the Graeme Souness revolution at Rangers in 1988. He was part of the Premier Division winning team at Ibrox in his first season, featuring in 14 games as he helped ensure the Dons had to settle for second place at the start of the Govan men's nine in a row run. He went on to have a short spell playing under Mark McGhee at Reading before playing more than 100 games for Dunfermline between 1991 and 1996.

In 1996 Cooper made his first venture into management when he took charge of Ross County in the Third Division. The Scottish Football League newcomers had big ambitions and needed a big personality to fulfil those aims. Cooper did not disappoint, winning the Third Division title in 1999 before clinching promotion from the Second Division the following season. Under Cooper the Highland club became an established force in the First Division but his own high expectations took their toll, with the Dons legend resigning in 2002 due to the pressures of the job. Alex Ferguson was one of the first to offer his support, taking Cooper south to Manchester United's training base to get him back on the pitch coaching the Old Trafford stars.

That stint back under his old mentor's wing helped reignite Cooper's passion for management and he was appointed by Hartlepool United in 2003, earning an enviable reputation in the English game when he took the north-east outfit to the League One play-offs. Cooper was dismissed by Hartlepool in 2005 but was in demand and was hired by Gillingham later that year for a six month stint in charge. He returned to the north-east of Scotland after that experience and joined former Highland rival Steve Paterson on the Peterhead coaching staff in 2006, acting as assistant to the former Caley Thistle and Aberdeen boss before taking charge late in 2007 as manager. Cooper's early experiences with Aberdeen have transferred to his coaching career. He said: "I was 16 when I played my first game for Aberdeen, 17 when I scored in the Scottish Cup final win and 19 when we won in Europe. At the time I took it all in my stride but looking back now I appreciate most players will go through their whole career without those experiences. It meant a lot to me that someone like Alex Ferguson showed faith in me when I was starting out and I'll always be grateful for that. I took it into management with me - I've always believed in giving players a chance at 16 or 17 if they deserve it."

without exception, the entire Gothenburg team turned their hand to coaching at various levels

Ferguson has had a hand in the managerial careers of all of the Gothenburg greats who went down that particular road, sometimes direct and sometimes subtle. In the case of Eric Black, it was to provide a hint at what lay in store. When the rookie settled down behind his desk after taking control at Motherwell in 2001, he was greeted with a card from his former Dons boss which read simply: "Welcome to the rat's world."

Black and Ferguson had not parted on good terms at Pittodrie but the mutual respect survived the passage of time. Having retired at the age of 28, while with Metz in France, Black's switch to coaching was immediate as he embarked on securing qualifications on the continent and back in Scotland. He was appointed by the SFA to take charge of the national under-21 side and in 1998 joined Celtic's coaching staff to assist Jo Venglos. He also served under John Barnes at Parkhead before branching out on his own with the Motherwell manager's job in 2001. He went on to join Gary McAllister at Coventry City, as assistant manager, before stepping up to take the top job in 2003. Despite protests from the Coventry fans, Black was replaced by Peter Reid in the summer of 2004 but his qualities ensured employment was not an issue and he became Steve Bruce's assistant at Birmingham City before following him to Wigan Athletic late in 2007.

Without exception, the entire Gothenburg team turned their hand to coaching at various levels and in various positions. Doug Rougvie's career in that department was confined to the north-east, where he has now settled into a career in the North Sea oil industry. After his 1984 switch to Chelsea he went on to play for Brighton, Shrewsbury and Fulham before joining Dunfermline in 1989. After a season in Fife he and former Dons team-mate Chic McLelland joined forces as co-managers of Montrose and won promotion to the First Division with the Angus club in 1991. After leaving the Gable Endies in 1992 he returned to playing with the dominant Huntly side in the Highland League and later became manager at Christie Park, leading the club to the title in 1997. He also managed Cove Rangers before bowing out of coaching to concentrate on his career outside of the game.

Goal hero John Hewitt is another who has carved out a niche for himself in the north-east business world since his days as a player and coach. Hewitt, an accomplished golfer, had two spells on loan at Middlesborough during his post-Aberdeen spell with Celtic and also played for St Mirren as well as a stint in charge of Irish side Dundalk. He also assisted Rougvie at Cove Rangers but is now a materials manager in the oil and gas industry.

Miller remains the only hero from Sweden to have inherited the Dons hot-seat once occupied so convincingly by Ferguson, even if his tenure ended in the pain and ignominy of dismissal after 36 months. Miller led his side to second place in the league and cup in his first season in charge but felt that was not good enough and set about rebuilding a team he had once been part of. Ultimately his efforts failed and he walked away from the club to begin another rebuilding job, piecing his life back together in exile from Pittodrie for the first time since joining the club as a schoolboy.

Miller devoted his attentions to business interests in the city and soon embarked on a burgeoning career in the media as a broadcaster and newspaper columnist. Then, in 2004, the call from chairman Stewart Milne came. The legendary former captain was invited to join the board and, after intensive discussions, accepted.

At first he was determined to avoid the director of football tag, initially favouring the 'executive football consultant' moniker, as he attempted to reinforce the message that he had no interest in getting directly involved in first team affairs. He said at the time: "Don't call me the director of football, I don't want that. Initially, I was against being a director, but when I sat down and looked at the job role and the fact you require influence at the very top, I came around to seeing the merits of being a director. When I said I didn't want to be a director I meant I didn't want to just go to two board meetings in a month as that would not change anything. I wanted a role that could influence and change things, to make the club better."

His first act was to appoint Jimmy Calderwood to replace Steve Paterson and it proved an inspired piece of business. Calderwood, a former school select team-mate of his director of football, was given early encouragement that the balance of power was in his favour. Miller said: "He will be his own man. He will not have to run anything past me. I don't want to be a baby-sitter. I want to do the job which I have been asked to do, which is to look at all aspects of the football side from the bottom right up to the top. It will be the manager's role to look after the team. He will talk to me from time to time, hopefully not a lot. There will be no interference from me. I have been in the role of manager, I know what is required, I understand the role. I don't want to be manager here. Anyone who thinks that is off their head."

Miller has grown into the role on the Pittodrie board, gradually coming to accept the director of football billing and at ease with his position as an all-seeing presence around the ground. He attracted Lenny Taylor, the man so lauded by Neil Simpson and his generation, to head the youth academy as he tackles the important issue of restarting the conveyor belt of talent which the club built its success on. Miller also handles contract negotiations and acts as a buffer between Calderwood and the board.

The job has evolved, Miller's confidence has returned. When he was appointed he said: "To repair this will take time. It will not happen overnight. I will have to ask for patience from the fans – that is vital. They have been amazingly patient over recent years. I will hope they will afford me the same patience to take a look at the club and to implement changes."

The return to European competition in 2007, and the all-important qualification to the Uefa Cup group stages to earn ties against Panathinaikos, Lokomotiv Moscow, Atletico Madrid and Copenhagen, was the sign that the period for patience had passed and that results were being delivered. The legacy of Gothenburg lives on in the desire for success among the greats who still grace Pittodrie with their presence.

SEMI-FINAL FIRST LEG, ABERDEEN v WATERSCHEI
APRIL 6, 1983: ABERDEEN 5, WATERSCHEI 1

THE momentous victory over Bayern Munich was the turning point in the European run for Aberdeen. Until the final whistle the Dons faithful dared to dream of triumphing in the competition – but defeating the Germans created an air of expectancy in the Granite City.

Some bookmakers immediately installed Alex Ferguson's men at odds of 2-1 to win the trophy and the supporters had as much faith, rushing out to book trips to the final in Gothenburg in the hours that followed the quarter-final. Even though the semi-final draw had not been made the groundswell of opinion was that Aberdeen were on the march to the Ullevi.

Ferguson said: "Having beaten Bayern my players now have the confidence they need to go to the final. The younger lads were nervous, but it was a great experience for them. We have nothing to fear after defeating Bayern – and the other clubs left in the cup don't have a player like Karl-Heinze Rummenigge."

Scotland manager Jock Stein, a man who knew the road to European glory from his time leading Celtic, was in the crowd of 24,500 to witness the drama first hand. Stein

● Willie Miller leads Aberdeen out to face Waterschei at Pittodrie.

claimed: "There are no reasons at all why Aberdeen should not go all the way now. They have proved they can beat the best in Europe and it doesn't matter at all who they come up against in the semi-final."

Even the Bayern party were magnanimous in defeat, with captain Paul Breitner admitting: "We played as well as we could and we thought the game was over when we were 2-1 up with less than a quarter of an hour to go - but Aberdeen still had some strength in reserve. In my opinion they are good enough to win this cup, I hope they do."

Club president Willi Hoffman added: "I've been associated with the club for many years now, but I don't think we have had a harder game against any club. Aberdeen must be the best side in Europe at the moment and they have the ability and fight needed to lift the cup."

Thoughts immediately turned to the draw for the last four, which was scheduled to take place two days after the Bayern tie. Ferguson said: "Before we drew Bayern I was hoping to get Austria Vienna – but they have just put the holders, Barcelona, out, so they are a force all right.

"I don't think I would thank you for Waterschei. Anderlecht have not beaten them for four years and Waterschei have put Anderlecht out of the Belgian Cup for the last three years. I've had reports that they are unbeatable at home."

Real Madrid joined the Dons, Vienna and Waterschei in the hat. It was the "unbeatable" Belgians who were plucked out alongside the spirited Scots. Madrid were being quoted as favourites but there was a quiet air of confidence surrounding Aberdeen.

Ferguson, after learning of his side's test against Watershei, said: "We don't know too much about them so we will have to get to Belgium as soon as possible. Having beaten Bayern Munich we have no-one to fear. We will prepare for this semi-final as though we are about to meet the best team in the world. They are obviously a good side with some remarkable results in Europe behind them, but we will have an idea of what to expect once we watch them."

The draw, held in Zurich and attended by Aberdeen vice-chairman Chris Anderson, allowed the latest travel operation to spring into action and the clamour for semi-final tickets to begin.

The Red Army were creating waves themselves, earning praise and plaudits from

Grampian Police and others for their exemplary behaviour. The only blot on the copybook was a fan ejected from Pittodrie when he shook his umbrella too vigorously after a disputed refereeing decision and the shaft broke, flying onto the pitch. Even the police saw the funny side, allowing the fan back in after hearing his explanation.

Bayern Munich needed no introduction but, when the semi-final draw was made, the Dons fans could have been forgiven for scratching their heads and reaching for their atlas.

They wouldn't find Waterschei on any map though, with the distinctively named side hailing from the town of Genk in Belgium's mining region.

The club had a multi-national background and the squad Aberdeen lined up against in 1983 stayed true to that tradition by including players from Germany, Iceland, the Netherlands and Hungary.

● Belgian mascot Dorus Vanderhovwem added some colour to Pittodrie

Thor Waterschei, to give the club its full name, had emerged as a force in Belgian football under the shrewd guidance of German coach Ernst Kunnecke.

Among his key players were Belgian international Eddy Voordeckers and young Icelandic striker Larus Gudmundsson – who had netted five times in five European appearances – as well as the club's Danish skipper Pierre Janssen.

The relatively unknown and unglamorous opposition did not dent the enthusiasm of the Pittodrie masses. Supporters queued overnight, clutching the vouchers issued at previous domestic matches, to get their

The captains exchange pennants (top left), Neil Simpson (top right) and Eric Black (bottom left) celebrates before earning and embrace from Stuart Kennedy (centre) as the Aberdeen supporters enjoy the occasion.

● The Aberdeen players join the crowds as tickets for the semi-final go on sale.

hands on tickets for the first leg in Aberdeen. By the time the ticket office opened at 9am the line snaked the full length of the main stand and wrapped around the Beach End.

According to Archie Knox, who had watched Waterschei in action, the capacity crowd would be needed to spur Aberdeen on. Knox claimed the Belgians were better organised than Bayern Munich and visiting coach Kunnecke was confident about his own side's chances.

The German manager watched the Dons in action twice prior to his side's visit to Scotland and saw them beaten by St Mirren and Dundee United. Those performances gave him great hope, with Kunnecke claiming: "The way the Aberdeen back four are playing, I think we might well be able to catch them square on the break and get a goal from either Gudmundsson or Voordeckers, who both have a fair turn of speed.

"Also, I do not think Aberdeen will relish our man marking system. April 6 and April 19 will be the greatest days in Waterschei's history … we do not intend to make a mess of them. If we can snatch one goal at Pittodrie I will go back to Belgium a very happy man – they surely cannot score enough to put the tie out of our reach.

How wrong can one man be? The tie was not just out of reach after the first leg, Waterschei's chances of success had been blasted off the face of the planet.

Alex Ferguson distanced himself from Waterschei's pre-match posturing, his message was simple. The Dons manager said: "We have got to show Waterschei all the confidence that comes from beating a team like Bayern. We have got to show them the experience we picked up from those games against Bayern and it will be up to the lads to go out there and do another magnificent job for the club and fans. We simply have to stamp our confidence and ability all over the Belgians."

Quite simply, mission accomplished.

RAMPANT DONS HAVE BELGIANS IN A SPIN

ABERDEEN	5
WATERSCHEI	1

● *By Alastair Macdonald*

ABERDEEN are surely assured of a place in the European Cup Winners' Cup final in Gothenburg on May 11 after efficiently snuffing out the Belgian challenge of Waterschei in the first leg of their semi-final tie at Pittodrie last night.

Waterschei came to Scotland as something of an unknown quantity but on the evidence of last night's display I cannot see them making much impression on the four goal lead which the Dons seized with masterful assurance.

Aberdeen, given the impetus of a fairytale start, with two goals in the opening four minutes, were in command for most of the 90 minutes. Although the Belgians were dangerous on the break, they did not seriously threaten the Pittodrie rearguard.

A perfectionist might carp at the Dons losing a goal, which in the event of an overall draw would count double in Waterschei's favour, but the chance of that eventually arising seems remote.

● Eric Black tucks away the opener for the Dons.

Aberdeen manager Alex Ferguson's decision to bring Doug Bell back into his line up for this game was fully vindicated – and for just the reason which persuaded the Aberdeen manager to make the change.

Bell was a constant threat to the Belgian defence with his long, mazy runs and he was instrumental in two of the goals.

Following the Dons' early scoring burst there was a drop in the tempo and almost the danger of the home side finding themselves in a rut and unable to get out of it.

A two-goals-in-two-minutes spell early in the second half, however, dispelled any doubts and after Waterschei had notched their consolation goal the Dons matched it with their fifth counter.

The spread of the Aberdeen scoring – Eric Black, Neil Simpson, Peter Weir and Mark McGhee (2) all contributed to the tally – indicated how much of a team triumph this was.

The difference in class between the two sides was most evident in the number of times the Belgians were dispossessed by the sharper tackling of their Aberdeen counterparts – the two early goals both resulted from such incidents.

BLACK MAGIC GIVES DONS GREAT START

ABERDEEN made a dream start with a goal in 1 minute 20 seconds. Rougvie dispossessed Voordeckers on the right touchline and sent Bell away on a solo run. Bell resisted a couple of tackles in a penetrative run through the Belgian defence before squaring the ball in the goalmouth for BLACK to tap into the net.

Better followed in four minutes when SIMPSON dispossessed Bialousz on the edge of the penalty box and resisted a challenge before finding the net with a 15-yard drive.

Waterschei's first real raid in six minutes saw Voordeckers produce a clever back header from a Rolland Janssen free kick but the ball was wide of target.

Three minutes later a snap shot by Bell was deflected for a corner by Clijsters.

The first real danger from the Belgian side came in 13 minutes when Martos broke on the right touchline. His cross was taken on the volley by Voordeckers but the ball went into the side netting.

A minute later Leighton parried a Gudmundsson shot and a Voordeckers try from the rebound was blocked by McLeish.

Back at the other end a Black shot on the turn was deflected over the bar.

The Belgians, however, were moving well when they did get an attack in motion.

It was the Dons, however, who were the more aggressive side and in 24 minutes Bell sent a 25-yarder over the bar from a short free kick by Weir.

Three minutes later the Dons came within inches of increasing their lead. A Strachan free kick on the right found McLeish beyond the far post and the central defender's powerful header beat Pudelko only to rebound from the face of the keeper's left-hand upright.

On the half-hour mark a long clearance by Miller sent Black clear on a run through the middle and Pudelko did well to beat down the Aberdeen striker's parting shot.

Waterschei continued to be dangerous in spasmodic bursts and in one of these in 37 minutes Leighton finger-tipped a swerving free kick from Pierre Janssen over the bar.

This sparked off a series of three corners in quick succession but the Aberdeen goal survived the onslaught.

A Strachan cross in 42 minutes produced a melee in the Waterschei goalmouth.

Just on the interval Roland Janssen flighted a free kick from outside the box but the ball passed just over the bar.

The Dons almost started the second half as they had the first with the Waterschei goal having two narrow escapes in the opening two minutes.

Only a brilliant flying save by Pudelko enabled the Belgian keeper to palm a Black header from a Kennedy cross round the post.

Black again got his head to the ball from Weir's flag kick but this time Van Kraay was waiting on the goal line to clear.

In 52 minutes Black missed a good scoring chance when a lucky break of the ball left him

c Black hits the net.

possession. In attempting to a more favourable shooting ition, however, the young ker was dispossessed.

ypical Bell burst from deep in Aberdeen defence in 59 utes took him to the edge of Belgian penalty box where he d up the ball for McGhee to get shot which Pudelko gathered y at the second attempt.

Ghee was just off target with other 20-yard try three minutes er.

erdeen's outfield superiority s more adequately reflected en they scored a third goal in minutes. Bell again created the ening with a byline cross from e left and McGHEE nipped in turn the ball past Pudelko.

vo minutes later McGhee anged from goalscorer to almaker when his cross from

the right touch line saw WEIR find the net with a diving header.

Waterschei substituted Ivo Plessers for Coenen in 70 minutes and the Belgians startled the Dons supporters with a goal four minutes later.

Voordeckers, Waterschei's most dangerous raider throughout the game, cut back the ball from the byline and GUDMONDSSON rose to head the ball into the net off the underside of the crossbar.

The Belgians immediately made a second substitution, Connix replacing Van Kraay.

Aberdeen made a double substitution in 78 minutes when Cooper and Hewitt replaced Bell and Black.

The Waterschei goal had a remarkable escape three minutes later when a Kennedy

cross from the byline ran along the goal-line with Cooper only inches away from making contact.

The Aberdeen goal machine, however, was still functioning and it was no surprise when they scored again in 84 minutes, McGHEE finally getting the ball in the net after having two shots blocked on the goal-line.

ABERDEEN – Leighton, Kennedy, Rougvie, Bell (Cooper), McLeish, Miller, Stracham, Simpson, McGhee, Black (Hewitt), Weir.

WATERSCHEI – Pudelko, Martos, Bialousz, David, Van Kraay (Connix), Coenen (E.Plessers), P. Janssen, Clijsters, Voordeckers, Gudmundsson, R. Janssen.

Referee – P. Bergamo, Italy.

SEMI-FINAL SECOND LEG, WATERSCHEI v ABERDEEN
APRIL 19, 1983: WATERSCHEI 1 ABERDEEN 0,

THREE goals were possible, five goals were beyond the wildest dreams of the Dons ahead of their semi-final first leg against Waterschei.

The resounding victory was as impressive as it was ruthless. The ease with which the Belgians were trampled over was expected but the margin was not.

Aberdeen vice-chairman Chris Anderson said: "It is a great night for the city of Aberdeen and the whole north of Scotland in fact. From what Alex Ferguson and Archie Knox had seen, we knew that the Waterschei defenders were slowish and sluggish and if we went at them we felt we could score two or three goals. We didn't expect five goals but it could have been seven or eight in the end."

Assistant manager Knox was also Ferguson's chief scout during the Euro mission. He had identified the continental rearguard as the weak link and was proved right on a sensational night.

Knox said: "After watching Waterschei twice I certainly thought we would get the desired result at Pittodrie – but not by 5-1. That is an exceptional scoreline in the semi-final of a European tournament. The Belgians' two front men played far better tonight than I thought they would but we thought if we put their defence under pressure right from the start it would pay dividends."

For Alex Ferguson the pieces of the cup jigsaw were falling into place with almost unnerving simplicity. The manager said: "We had a magnificent start and that changed things for them. I expected us to be nervous but the goals put us at ease. I could not have asked for more from my players. Doug Bell was magnificent and proved me right by his attitude throughout the game. In the second leg we must play to the Bayern plan that has proved so successful for us in the past. We must continue to threaten them as much as possible as their two strikers threatened us tonight."

While Ferguson tried to urge caution, there

was no doubt in the mind of the Waterschei camp about the way the two legged tie was going to end. Coach Ernst Kunnecke said: "It's finished. I don't think there is any team who could take four goals off Aberdeen this season. In fact, I feel it will be two or three years before I can have my team able to play in that kind of fashion."

There was a long list of dignitaries on the Pittodrie roll call for the Waterschei tie. Former England manager Sir Alf Ramsay, Scotland boss Jock Stein and a clutch of club coaches took their place in the main stand alongside Real Madrid assistant team chief Luis Molowny.

The Spaniard's assessment was frank, claiming: "I was very impressed by the power, strength and ability of Aberdeen – a team we do not know all that much about in Spain. If it turns out to be a Real versus Aberdeen final I would expect it to be very difficult for us judging by the Aberdeen tonight. The scoreline was a clear indication of the difference in standards between the two sides. As far as I can see the second leg will be a formality."

Sweden here we come!

● Dons fans in Belgium.

DONS UNLUCKY TO LOSE UNBEATEN TAG

WATERSCHEI	1
ABERDEEN	0

(Aggregate 2-5)

● *By Alastair Macdonald*

Aberdeen duly consolidated their place in the European Cup Winners' Cup final in Gothenburg on May 11 with a thoroughly professional performance before a 15,000 crowd in Genk's Dumont Stadium.

The only goal of the second leg of this semi-final fell to Waterschei, but the scoreline was a poor reflection of a game in which the Dons never lost control of the situation and might indeed have won by a goal or two on the basis of chances created.

The Belgian crowd, appeased by their team becoming the first to defeat Aberdeen in the current tournament, gave the Dons a standing ovation as they left the field.

Despite having to do without no fewer than four first choice players due to injury, the Aberdeen side met the challenge with calmness and resolve and, although their unbeaten record was broken, they can be eminently satisfied with the Genk result.

The goal which did the damage realised the reservations which the Aberdeen players had about the Belgian pitch when they viewed it on Monday night.

At that time they found it hard and bumpy, with bare patches here and there – one Aberdeen player likened it to a Belgian Cappielow – and overnight rain

● Mark McGhee dominates in the air

did little to improve its condition.

The uncertain bounce of the ball played a part in Waterschei's goal and both Willie Miller and Alex McLeish slipped before they could make a challenge on Eddy Voordeckers as the Belgian moved in to score the 73rd minute counter.

The goal came as the climax to a period of sustained pressure by Waterschei, but the reverse did not disturb the Dons' composure and it seemed more likely that they would equalise than that the Belgians would further reduce the four-goal deficit from the first leg.

The unhappy coincidence of Miller and McLeish both losing their footing was the only mistake, if it could be called that, that the Aberdeen central defensive pair made throughout the game, otherwise they provided an inspiring example of calmness and efficiency under pressure.

This was another fine team effort by the Dons and the players drafted into the side for this game all played their part.

The Dons even allowed themselves the luxury of fielding teenager Willie Falconer for his European debut when he appeared as a second-half substitute for Mark McGhee. A second Aberdeen substitution saw Ian Angus replace Neil Simpson a few minutes before the final whistle.

VOORDECKERS GRABS BELGIAN CONSOLATION

● Waterschei defender Pierre Plessers rises to clear the danger

In 10 minutes Hewitt, operating on the left with Weir on the right flank, made space for himself and sent in a right foot shot from 25 yards but Pudelko collected the ball just inside the left hand post.

Leighton's next call to action came in 13 minuts when he held a volley from Gudmundsson and Aberdeen immediately broke away to force the first corner of the game.

The Belgians continued to look unsure of themselves under pressure as Aberdeen put their policy of doing their defending in the opposition's half into practice.

A promising break through the middle by Simpson in 24 minutes ended with the Aberdeen player being crowded oout on the edge of the Waterschei penalty box.

Two minutes later Voordeckers sent a header over the bar from a Martos free kick but for the most part Aberdeen were winning the aerial duals in their goalmouth, with McLeish in particular dominating the area.

On the half hour Waterschei won their first corner but Leighton clutched Roland Janssen's flag kick cleanly.

ABERDEEN were first to attack and as in the first leg the Belgians were guilty of unforced errors in the opening minutes.

Waterschei, however, were first to get in a shot, first Pierre Plessers, and then Roland Janssen getting 25 yard shots on target but Leighton confidently fielded both efforts.

Miller had an admonitory finger waved at him by the East German referee in six minutes for a challenge on Van Kraay, the Dutchman making the most of the incident.

Waterschei were pressing hard for an early goal which could prove vital to their chances but their over anxiety was betrayed in Pierre Plessers sending a 30-yard free kick high over the bar.

Waterschei made an unexpected substitution in 37 minutes when Massignani replaced Gudmundsson. The Icelander did not seem to be injured but the change may have been tactical as the newcomer was soon in the thick of the action in Waterschei's attacks.

Rougvie made a brave attempt to convert a Weir cross into a goal in 39 minutes when he dived full length to meet the ball at the far post but goalkeeper Pudelko just beat him to it.

A minute later Weir was just wide of target with a 25 yard drive as the Dons increasingly gained command of the exchanges.

Just on the interval McGhee broke clear on his own from a Rougvie clearance but, after shaking off one challenge, the Aberdeen number nine was foiled by Pudelko, who ran from his goal to challenge.

Two minutes after the resumption Simpson almost put the Dons in front when his left foot shot from a Weir flag kick beat Pudelko but struck the base of the keeper's left hand upright.

The following minute Simpson and Hewitt both had tries parried and McGhee missed a golden scoring opportunity, sending the ball into the side netting with an open goal yawning in front of him.

Aberdeen continued to press and the Belgian goal had another narrow escape when a Rougvie header was cleared off the goal line by Van Kraay.

● Neil Simpson and Roland Janssen tangle in midfield

In 54 minutes a Belgian counter-attack saw Leighton hold a 30 yard shot from Ivo Plessers, but Aberdeen returned to the attack and Pudelko was almost caught out by a 30 yard free kick from McMaster. The keeper got down just in time to trap the ball on the goal line when the fierce grounder penetrated the Waterschei wall.

The Dons were playing with great confidence, combining cool possession football in midfield with sudden breaks forward, while the Belgian attacking efforts were more in hope than expectancy.

Leighton, however, had to move smartly in 64 minutes to hold a close range try from Massignani, and this sparked off a burst of pressure by the Belgian side, during which a Voordeckers header rebounded from the Aberdeen crossbar.

Waterschei's revival roused their supporters to fresh vocal efforts but Aberdeen were coping effectively.

There was an indication of this

when the Dons first substitution came in 71 minutes and it was a striker. Mark McGhee was replaced by teenager Willie Falconer, making his European debut.

Leighton produced a finger tip save from a close range effort by Roland Janssen but the Waterschei pressure was rewarded in 73 minutes when VOORDECKERS opened their account.

Miller and McLeish in quick succession both slipped in going to halt a forward run by the blond Belgian striker, who was eventually left free to run in and send the ball past the advancing Leighton.

Aberdeen's response was to return to the offensive and Falconer tested Pudelko with a shot from the right.

Back at the other end Leighton went full length to hold a grounder from Voordeckers.

With six minutes left for play, Aberdeen made a second substitution when Angus replaced Simpson.

WATERSCHEI – Pudelko, Martos, P. Plessers, David, Van Kraay, I. Plessers, P. Janssen, Clijsters, Voordeckers, Gudmundsson (Massignani), R. Janssen.

ABERDEEN – Leighton, Kennedy, Rougvie, McMaster, McLeish, Miller, Hewitt, Simpson (Angus), McGhee (Falconer), Watson, Weir.

MOBILISING THE RED ARMY

REAL MADRID, on course to be crowned champions of Spain ahead of closest challengers Valencia, were running scared. Assistant manager Luis Molowny was in Genk to watch Aberdeen book their place in the European Cup Winners' Cup final and what he saw was enough to persuade boss Alfredo di Stefano to accompany his sidekick to Pittodrie the following Saturday, when the Dons returned to domestic duty with a league match against Hibs.

While Molowny was impressed, the Pittodrie management left Belgium with a slight tinge of regret despite the magical outcome of the two leg semi-final against Waterschei. Alex Ferguson said: "Losing our undefeated record was a disappointment." The hardest of task masters did relent slightly to add: "We're delighted to be in a European final."

Delight did not come close to summing up the feelings of the Aberdeen fans who were heading for football wonderland. All they had to do was get there.

They landed on Swedish shores in their hundreds, descended on the country's airports in their thousands and turned Gothenburg into a Scottish colony. The mobilisation of the Red Army was like nothing that had ever been seen in the Granite City and it turned into an operation planned with military precision.

The team, the most precious cargo of all, had to be settled into their Scandinavian holding camp and the legions of supporters also had to be temporarily relocated in their pursuit of the holy grail of a European trophy.

One of the prime architects of the mission was Glasgow-based businessman Harry Hynds, the official Dons travel agent during that glittering era. Hynds and his company no longer handle the Aberdeen arrangements but that does not dilute his pride in the part he played in the in the adventure.

He said: "We took 2,500 people to Gothenburg on 20 aircraft. The planes came from everywhere, they had to. We had some from Thomson Holidays, from Dan-Air … anyone who had a spare aircraft on that date was called upon to help out. The team plane had The Flying Dons emblazoned on the nose. The club and I were presented with a replica of the plane and mine is at home, safe and sound.

"It was obviously a great commercial relationship between the club and I but really finances weren't the main motivation, it was a privilege to be involved in such an exciting time for the club and the city. The company mainly handles Celtic trips now but I still look out for the Aberdeen results every week. It was an amazing period in football history for Aberdeen."

Hynds helped Aberdeen every step of the way, from the preliminary round tie against Switzerland in Sion to the climax in Sweden, and there were some eventful journeys along the way. High on that list was the first round fixture against Dinamo Tirana, when the Glaswegian found himself filling an unexpected role as roving television

● Passengers on the St Clair (top and bottom) were joined by fellow sea going fans on some of the north-east fishing trawlers (middle) to make their way to Gothenburg. Other enterprising fans (right) took to the roads to reach Sweden in time for the game.

reporter as concerns about a potential military coup intensified.

He said: "There were some great adventures on the run to Gothenburg. The trip to Albania came just a few days after a heavily armed group had been shot by security forces while they tried to land a boat as part of a suspected coup and there were some dramatic headlines at the time. In actual fact it was a very smooth trip and the hospitality was first class, but I ended up becoming Grampian Television's man in Albania and reporting back to the studio in Aberdeen.

I had to tell them that all of the fears about unrest were unfounded, which may not have been the type of exciting news they had expected.

"We took a 119 seat aircraft for the game against Tirana but carried only 19 people from the club and a handful of press - that meant only a few people saw Dougie Bell's performance, when he must have lost about two stone in weight covering every blade of grass that night. It was a completely different story for so many of the European games I was involved in during our time working with Aberdeen, taking four or five

Dick was a gentleman through and through, an absolute one off

planes to Munich and the same to Hamburg for those ties."

The massed journeys to Germany were nothing compared to the Gothenburg exercise, a project which tested Hynds and his staff to the limit as they struggled to cope with the demand created by an expectant Dons support. The Aberdeen fans were not the only ones brimming with optimism – the club's travel agent had started to believe a European final appearance was possible long before the Dons had reached the latter stages of the tournament. Plans for Aberdeen's appearance in Gotheburg were in place while the team was still negotiating the early rounds.

Hynds said: "We did all the travel for the club, from the supporters to the team and officials. We actually started booking accommodation for Gothenburg as early as September. I wouldn't say it was blind optimism - the team was playing so well and the manager had a midas touch.

"I dealt primarily with the chairman, Dick Donald. He was an unbelievable man, a true gentleman and he was a huge loss to football when he died. Dick was a gentleman through and through, an absolute one off. We all know the reputation Aberdonians have when it comes to money but the chairman had a fantastic attitude, he told me that he didn't mind what it cost as long as he got the best for his team and the best for the supporters. He and Chris Anderson were wonderful to deal with.

"The first time we were involved with Aberdeen was in 1981 when we dealt with the travel for the Uefa Cup tie against Ipswich. We flew into an RAF base nearby and it was a good trip, so our link snowballed from there. We spent 13 years as the club's official travel agent.

"There were challenges along the way but we always overcame them. At that time there was no flexibility with Aberdeen airport - the doors closed at 9.30pm and that was that. It meant we had to stay on after evening games and even for matches during the day it was a sweat to get back in time."

Football's image in the 1980s was not clean cut. Problems with hooliganism had plagued the game, particularly during the European excursions of English clubs, but there were no problems associated with Aberdeen's invasion of Gothenburg. The Dons fans travelled in high spirits but their conduct was praised by the Swedish authorities. Hynds had the onerous task of taking responsibility for the thousands who travelled bearing his company's name on their tickets.

He said: "We carried 2,500 people and the only problem we encountered was when one supporter decided to test the sprinkler system in his hotel room in Gothenburg on the eve of the game. It worked. Mind you, he paid for the damage with a smile on his face after the result the next day and the Aberdeen fans were absolutely fantastic. Their behaviour was superb throughout the run.

"I was in Sweden to control what was a huge exercise for my team. I remember being invited to the official reception after the final and remarking that it wasn't just Aberdeen who had a winning team - I did too. At that time it was a team of 12 at the company and we managed to ticket 2,500 people in the weeks between qualifying and the final."

The logistics of flying thousands of football fans to Scandinavia was only part of the conundrum for Hynds and his team. Finding somewhere for the masses to sleep was another part, during what was an eventful time in his own personal life. The test was passed with flying colours, with only two members of the travelling army left to rough it.

He said: "My son, Iain, was due to be born around that time and my wife and I were in a bit of panic because we had been told he could arrive early. As it happened, his birthday is June 30 so we had plenty of time to spare but it was a nervous time for us when I was out in Sweden. Fortunately it passed without incident and I was back in plenty of time.

"Professionally it also went to plan. When we travelled to Gothenburg originally we spoke to various hotels and asked to book the rooms. We went back and forth a few times to make sure we had enough accommodation for everyone who wanted to travel and we were able to do that. Myself and Ian Hardie, who was my second in command, slept on the floor of a meeting room in the Europa Hotel on the night of the game because there were no spare rooms for us once the fans had been accommodated. It was a good night's sleep after a few libations."

Housing the supporters was a big part of the operation but arguably not the most important. The other key role was locating a hideaway for the VIPs who made the trip. The Aberdeen team members were the men at the centre of the most carefully executed travel operation, with Hynds personally seeking out the ideal pre-final bolthole for Ferguson and his troops.

The agent said: "The manager and the directors left it in my hands but I knew they were perfectionists and the travel arrangements had to meet their standards. I've seen a few sides to Alex Ferguson but you have to say he is a true master at what he does. Usually you would beat a hasty retreat when he began clearing his throat for one of his outbursts, but I have to say he was very calm during that run and such a professional to deal with.

"When it came to choosing the team a place to stay, I travelled across and found the Hotel Fars Hatt, which is around 18 kilometres outside of Gothenburg. The city was going to be far too busy with fans so the location in the countryside was ideal, with a lovely spot on the water front and lots of peace and quiet for the players. In fact, its still going strong 25 years on. As soon as I visited the hotel I called back to Pittodrie and said they had to take it - for one thing it was a great hotel but it also had a perfect Doric name!"

The Fars Hatt, which translates to Father's Hat, remains a popular holiday destination in Sweden. Located just a 15 minute drive north of Gothenburg, the hotel prides itself on its peaceful location close to the Nordre River. It began life in 1684 as an eight-room inn but has now grown to boast 120 rooms as well as an outdoor swimming pool and a host of other leisure facilities.

Even in 1983 the hotel, which had received a glowing recommendation from a security guard the Aberdeen manager had befriended during pre-season visits to Sweden, was considered a luxurious option. The Real Madrid team in contrast were housed in a city hotel which was past its best.

More than 40 flights departed from Aberdeen airport while the shipping lanes were also busy, with several trawlers making the journey from the north-east to Scandinavia. Dedicated duo Ian Annal and Neil McCallum travelled by motorbike, taking a week to make the round trip.

The travelling army of Dons fans snapped up the bulk of the accommodation in

Gothenburg having finalised their logistics. Others took advantage of their own floating hotel, commandeering the P&O ferry St Clair for the sea crossing to Scandinavia. The company recognised the perfect opportunity to put its fleet member to good use as the demand for transport quickly outstripped supply and spaces onboard were quickly snapped up to justify the decision to re-route the ship for its special one-off assignment.

it was 1992 before the St Clair, an icon of the Gothenburg final, was finally replaced by P&O

Close to 500 high spirited followers crammed onto the vessel for the journey and the St Clair became a focal point for the final, providing the perfect photo opportunity as newspapers and television crews clamoured to demonstrate the scale of the exodus from the Granite City in the build-up to the final and a giant floating party venue for the triumphant return leg after the success against Real Madrid.

● The St Clair sets sail for Sweden from Aberdeen harbour.

The voyage continued the amazing scenes which had bemused yet enchanted the Swedes as their Scottish guests marked the club's first continental trophy in style and when the St Clair berthed back in the calm waters of Aberdeen harbour the exuberance showed no signs of abating, with joyous fans spilling onto the quayside and making their way into the heart of a city that was in the grip of the type of unity never seen before or since.

The boat had first arrived in Scottish waters in 1977 when it was pressed into action on the Shetland to Aberdeen route, the first roll-on roll-off ferry the island had seen. It made the journey three times a week and was classed as the finest ship ever to serve the north, measuring 123 metres by 18 metres, but it was its role in the Gothenburg expedition which won it a special place in maritime history.

The St Clair IV, to give it its full title, dated back to 1965 when it began life as the Peter

Pan on the Travemünde to Trelleborg route in Sweden having been built in Germany. Six years later the ship moved to Britain, renamed the SF Peter Pan, to patrol the Southampton to San Sebastian beat for a four year stint ahead of its lengthy service on the Aberdeen to Lerwick route. It was 1992 before the St Clair, an icon of the Gothenburg final, was finally replaced by P&O and can now be found in warmer climes, serving as a troop ship for the Malaysian army under her new name Nusa Pejuang.

In 1983 the St Clair, captained by Dons supporter Mike Gray, set sail from Aberdeen on Monday, May 9, having had a fitting send off from the Grampian Police Pipe Band. The voyage began at 1.30pm and took 26-hours, with a programme of entertainment hosted by television's Ron Dale which included music from resident duo Aquarius as well as feature films, football skill competitions and bingo. There were, of course, the St Clair bars to keep passengers occupied in between and in excess of 14,000 cans of lager were consumed by the 493 fans who made the trip.

On the day of the game, a fleet of 11 coaches transported ferry passengers to the stadium and were primed an ready to speed the triumphant Dons fans back to the vessel after the final whistle. In the early hours of May 12 the St Clair left Gothenburg behind and the floating party headed for home.

Scott Colegate was the passenger manager tasked with solving the logistical puzzle of transporting hundreds of football fans to Sweden. Now an admistrator with Scottish Hydro Contractors in Aberdeen, Colegate recalls: "I was at the game and had the task of getting the 11 coaches back to the St Clair organised. The supporters from the ship were due to be sitting together but some were moved because of the bad weather and because of that we had passengers coming out of different exits and I had to run around the outside of the stadium trying to pick out the ones who should be travelling with us.

"We had quite a few people who had been thrown off various flights trying to hitch a lift with us, climbing up the mooring ropes as we left - that made things interesting for a while, but we got away with only the people who should have been onboard.

"It was a journey of celebration but it was also a poignant one. In the early stages of the voyage there was a two minute silence as a mark for respect for Philip Goodbrand, our passenger who died during the match at the Ullevi. There was also a collection for his family and he was in everyone's thoughts, even amid the celebrations."

Alex Ferguson and Mark McGhee were waiting on the quayside to greet the homecoming fans and to parade the European Cup Winners' Cup. There were joyous scenes at the end of a journey which had gone perfectly to plan, despite concerns about the brave P&O service from the beginning.

Eric Turner was the P&O general manager who had the courage to approve the proposal to use the St Clair for the run to Gothenburg and he was rewarded with impeccable behaviour by the Red Navy, as the seagoing supporters became known. There were security officers on the ship but there was need, with not even a hint of trouble despite the high spirits. Future requests by the Old Firm to run similar services to continental ties were always rejected, with the company not so confident that the Glasgow fans could maintain the high standards set by their Dons counterparts.

Colegate said: "The BBC had a television crew on board and the feeling was that they were hoping to capture some fighting or trouble. That didn't materialise - it was a carnival atmosphere on the St Clair. There was a good mix of passengers, including grannies and children, so it was all good natured fun. We knew what we were getting with Dons fans and we had been careful to select passengers with Aberdeen addresses, hoping that would help everyone get along. The nearest we came to any conflict was when Ron Dale burst into a rendition of 'I Belong to Glasgow'. Needless to say, he was confronted by what seemed like all 500 passengers pointing at him and chanting 'You what, You what' at him. You could see the sweat on his brow but he turned it round by finishing with The Northern Lights."

Colegate has also revealed that a remote branch of the Aberdeen supporters' club had a key role to play in ensuring the hundreds of fans who took advantage of the St Clair's capacity were able to make the overseas excursion.

He said: "If we were going to disrupt Shetland's lifeline service by taking the St Clair off her usual route, it had to be done with the blessing of the islanders and we certainly had that. A group of 60 Aberdeen supporters from Shetland were on the ship and that really was the key to making the whole thing happen. After Gothenburg we branched out and did a few different mini-cruises to Holland, Germany and Scandinavia. Again, as long as we were catering for the Shetlanders there were never any complaints.

"I spent 36 years with P&O and the Gothenburg adventure was by far the most memorable event of that career. It was something which was completely untried and which carried a certain risk - but we were always confident that the Aberdeen supporters wouldn't pose any problems."

FERGIE'S FINAL WORD!

● *Alastair Guthrie on the line from Gothenburg*

'My players will give their last ounce of energy to win the cup'

ABERDEEN today stand only one step away from entering European football's hall of fame.

Eight months and 10 gruelling ties have passed since the Dons embarked on their assault on Europe and the biggest prize in the club's history – the Cup Winners' Cup – is now tantalisingly lying at their fingertips.

And the path which has taken the Dons to diverse places such as Switzerland, Albania, Poland, West Germany and Belgium can finish in total glory with a win over the mighty Real Madrid here in Gothenburg.

Manager Alex Ferguson today spoke his last words on tonight's final as he counted away the minutes to kick-off in the Dons posh training complex in the picturesque Swedish countryside.

And the Dons boss is determined his players will return to a heroes welcome tomorrow with 16 glittering medals and a cup to show for their efforts and not just memories.

Ferguson was still cool and showing no signs of pre-match tension when he told me his final thoughts on tonight's meeting with Alfredo Di Stefano's legendary men in white.

"Yes, we have a marvellous chance to do it and I know each player will give his last ounce of energy to win the cup.

"We intend to play our normal game – and our normal game is to attack. It would be foolish if we were to suddenly try a pattern that is foreign to our nature.

"I don't believe the fact we are playing a big name club like Real is anything to do with it. We have already beaten Bayern Munich over 90 minutes and everyone in European football knows the reputation of the Germans.

"But if we go into tonight's match as underdogs we will finish up with memories instead of winners' medals. And we are not in Gothenburg to finish as losers."

Ferguson today took his cup final squad for a stroll among the Swedish pines before a light training session.

The Cup Winners' Cup has been taking pride of place in a huge department store within the city centre complex and Ferguson wants nothing more than to see skipper Willie Miller accept the trophy from UEFA president Artem Franchi tonight.

Captain Miller started his European career on a winning note nine years ago here in Gothenburg in an under-23 tie played only 100 yards from the venue for tonight's final the Ullevi Stadium.

And it would be fitting if he were to crown the club's greatest moment back in the Swedish seaport in his 55th successive game for the Dons this season.

Aberdeen, however, would not only be writing a new chapter for Pittodrie they would also alter the European record books if they beat Real.

For no club asked to play in a preliminary round has ever carried away this sparkling trophy in the tournament's 22-year history.

DOUG BELL AND STUART KENNEDY OUT OF FERGIE'S STARTING RECKONING BUT...

DONS BOSS FINDS A SILVER LINING...

● *Alastair Macdonald roports from Gothenburg*

FOR a football club manager being an optimist is almost a prerequisite occupational qualification.

Certainly the ability to look on the bright side is a quality which Aberdeen manager Alex Ferguson has had ample opportunity to explore during the Dons' injury-dogged build-up to the European Cup Winners' Cup final against Real Madrid in the Ullevi Stadium, Gothenburg tomorrow night.

Yesterday brought the double confirmation that Doug Bell is unlikely to take any part in the final after aggravating his recent ankle injury in a try out with the reserves in Edinburgh on Sunday and that Stuart Kennedy, although greatly improved, will have to content himself with a substitute's role.

Manager Ferguson, however, can find consolation for the real disappointment of both Kennedy and Bell being removed from the starting line-up reckoning in the quality of the players he has available as replacements.

"The injuries which have deprived us of players such as Stuart Kennedy, Doug Bell an[d] Eric Black in the last few week[s] have been a blow, but the fac[t] that they have happened whe[n] they did could prove to hav[e] been a blessing in disguise," sai[d] the Aberdeen manager.

"The players who have com[e] into the side as replacement[s] particularly John McMaster an[d] John Hewitt, have made th[e] most of their opportunity [to] settle down through getting in [a] few games in a row."

Manager Ferguson clearly do[es] not think his side have be[en] significantly weakened by t[he] injury problems.

"Who is to say what my best si[de] is for any particular game?" asks. "After all, with the pool [I] have at PIttodrie, there [are] always some good play[ers] having to be left out. There ha[ve] been times, for instance, whe[n I] have left Bell out of the side [for] tactical reasons."

Had Bell and Kennedy been [fit] I'm sure the Aberdeen mana[ger]

THE MEDIA

JIM DOLAN *was in Gothenburg for* The Press and Journal *on the night of Aberdeen's greatest triumph, though he did not know until a few days before that he was going to Sweden, since he was not the recognised Dons reporter, Alastair Macdonald being the man responsible for the Reds coverage at the time. But, fiddler's invitation or not, Jim found himself on a flight to Gothenburg on the morning of the European Cup-Winners' Cup final, a game that would set Alex Ferguson's name in the granite of Aberdeen forever.*

ould have had both in his starting line-up, but that could have meant McMaster dropping out and there is ample room for argument that, in opposition to Real Madrid's style of play, McMaster's accurate use of the ball could prove of greater value than Bell's forte of taking on the opposition at close quarters.

The Aberdeen manager will not name his side until tomorrow but, in the absence of Kennedy and Bell, it does not require profound insight to speculate that Doug Rougvie and McMaster will occupy the full back berths with Neale Cooper moving forward into the midfield.

The manager yesterday gave Gordon Strachan a vote of confidence as the team's penalty taker. He made it clear that Strachan would take any penalties awarded to Aberdeen during the game despite having failed with his last two spot-kick attempts.

Manager Ferguson confesses to a personal lack of excitement over tomorrow's final at the moment, but he is equally sure that the stomach butterflies will be fluttering in overdrive by the time the big game comes round.

His objective will be, of course, to conceal this from the players, and he is confident that there is sufficient experience of the big occasion spread over his squad to make this a comparatively minor problem.

"Some of the younger players may require some reassurance but that's all", he said today.

All that Mr Ferguson will be asking of the Aberdeen team tomorrow is that they again reach the heights of their performance in Munich a couple of months ago – not an easy task certainly but one within their powers.

Manager Ferguson does not find much to separate Bayern Munich and Real Madrid in terms of difficult opponents.

"Real have a busier midfield than Bayern in defensive terms, but the Spanish team's back four are not as disciplined as the West Germans. Real definitely have no Rummenigge, although Santillana will provide problems."

Real Madrid are still awaiting a final decision on whether Uli Stielike will be passed fit for the final. Manager Alfredo Di Stefano has already indicated that he will play the West German international if possible but this must be considered something of a gamble as the 28 year-old Steilike, who operates in midfield, missed the last five games.

In the one-upmanship contest which always precedes a game of this nature, the Spanish club feel they have scored over their Scottish rivals by securing a well-equipped sports centre outside Gothenburg for their headquarters but the Aberdeen party are quite happy in their country retreat.

It was great to be a Press and Journal reporter in season 1982-83, if only because of the reaction of the Glasgow sporting press when you arrived to cover a Dons game at Parkhead or Ibrox.

Mock abuse to the reporter from the north, the occasional curse and bitter disappointment was the usual fate of the Glasgow contingent as Fergies' boys would emerge with at least a draw but, more likely, a victory.

Alastair MacDonald was the Dons full-time reporter then, and I would come off the bench when he required a day off to cover an Aberdeen match. My other duties were to attend Celtic and Rangers games, other matches involving the Dons' future opponents as well as keeping an eye on Dundee United's progress in Europe and Premier Division.

I had a really good job then, though I probably did not fully appreciate it at the time, since it led to my covering Celtic, Rangers, Hearts, Hibs and Dundee United on various European forays. But the one and only job as far as any sports reporter on the P&J was concerned, was to be the Dons man.

Though I was more than likely to find myself bound for Kilmarnock or Partick for meaningless matches near the season's end, Alastair having surfeited himself on meetings with the Old Firm and any New Firm clashes that happened along, he did make way on occasion for "big" games.

That was when I was able to enjoy the discomfiture of the press gang from the centre of their universe, and I almost felt part of Fergie's team as they notched up another good result in the Glasgow manor. The fact that my club was Motherwell, my home town team, with a built-in antipathy to the big Glasgow pair and the sectarian baggage both supports clearly carried then, only added to my appreciation of what Fergie was doing for football.

My father, born and raised a Roman Catholic, was virulently anti-sectarian and rejoiced in any Dons success over the Old Firm, and when Aberdeen reached the European Cup Winners' Cup final could not have been happier. Mother, my dear Protestant ma, was the one who directed me to support my local team, for whom father did not care a lot, it must be said. But she became a Dons fan because I worked for the Press and Journal and she identified with me as part of any success they enjoyed, even though I was not the Dons man.

With only weeks to the final I took a copy of the Dons anthem for Gothenburg: "A European Song" down to Motherwell and we'd play it enthusiastically on a Saturday night, joining in heartily when the other side of the tape "The Northern Lights of old Aberdeen" was played. We were all Dons fans then, and they retained an affection for the team from the Granite City until the day they died.

Don't ask me how or why, but mother, despite never having "turned", i.e. becoming a Catholic, was a staunch member of the local Women's Catholic Guild and, indeed, even held office in it at one time.

But she would forget herself sometimes when she attended Saturday night bingo at the guild, when Aberdeen would have gone away from Celtic Park with another three points. And she would say to one of her Catholic chums: "Aberdeen did well the day, didn't they?" to be met with groans from her green-tinted specs wearing friends. But it did give her a chance to say, on occasion: "Oor Jim was covering the game", which is what the purpose of her "forgetfulness" could have been all about. Which would explain her wicked wee smile when she would tell me about it.

My relationship with Alex Ferguson could be brittle at the time, since when I covered Dons matches I tended to look at them through a more critical lens than did Alastair, and it was not too rare an occasion that I would lift the telephone receiver in the morning to hear Mr Ferguson begin an obligatory football discussion, sometimes prefaced with the words: " Aye, you, ya…..".

My situation was not helped by the fact that one of my early stories, in Alex's first season in charge, was to produce a heavily critical comparison between Fergie's league record to date and the one compiled by predecessor Billy McNeill under the heading: "What's gone wrong with the Dons?"

It even had a chart comparing the performances of the Dons teams and it set a tone that would be difficult to soften as the years rolled by. Maybe I was too critical, or maybe I even helped Fergie become more successful than he might have been, though I doubt if the Dons boss would have seen it that way.

It was not the only time over the years I would be in hot water with an Aberdeen management team, which I put down to the fact that I was not an Aberdeen supporter, but an Aberdeen reporter, an explanation that failed to satisfy any of them.

In fairness to Alex Ferguson, he never held a grudge, but I think he breathed a little easier when he knew Alastair was covering games rather than me, and particularly if the game ended in defeat. And that's not knocking Alastair, an Aberdeen supporter, who was living the dream with every other fan and saw very little to criticise in the light of what had gone on prior to Fergie's arrival. Given the Dons success under Alex Ferguson, who is to say they were not right to modify the criticism?

Anyway, let's say Fergie and I tended to keep a respectable distance from each other at the time, and though it got a bit warmer as the years went by, we were never what you would call close. That's not to say the man did not show me kindnesses when he became Manchester United boss. Not mighty favours, by any means, but welcome gestures he did not really have to provide.

But, back to Gothenburg and that wonderful result. The build-up had been the usual one, with Fergie saying the boys could do it, but I suspect very few Aberdonians really thought the Dons would beat Real Madrid in the final and the vast majority went over there to party, win lose or draw, knowing instinctively that such an occasion was highly unlikely ever to be repeated.

I was involved only to the extent that I worked for the Press and Journal and covered some matches, rather like a supersub, and had been told there were no plans to include me in the final coverage, given that there was a team of news people and photographers going over who would mop up the news side of things.

Imagine my surprise when word came down from on high that I should make my way to Aberdeen airport for an early morning flight the day of the final, my job being to do the after-match quotes. Someone, a printer, I think, had fallen out, and there was a place on a flight for me.

the aircraft was full to the brim with a vast assortment of Dons fans

I had a job the night before in an Aberdeen hotel as master of ceremonies for an amateur boxing show as well as working for the paper. It was a night mixed with work and a modicum of alcohol and did not finish until the early hours of the morning, by which time a lot of aqua vitae had flowed under the bridge...of the nose.

So I was not best pleased the good lady wife announced suddenly, in the middle of the night, that my taxi was waiting outside. I had thrown some stuff hastily into a travel bag some time the night before, so it was quickly

● The first group of Aberdeen supporters touch down at Gothenburg's airport.

grabbed, shouldered and I was off to the airport.

It was pandemonium at the airport, with fans milling about in a red sea of excitement and agitation. I knew I was flying on a Scandinavian Air Service flight, a giant aircraft, and had an arrangement to meet Alastair Macdonald at a pre-arranged spot in Gothenburg, where we would duly received accreditation for the final , a nice sports holdall and goodie items from the nice people there.

The aircraft was full to the brim with a vast assortment of Dons fans. There craggy lads with Dons' tops and scarves that had seen better days, middle class couples from the nicer parts of Aberdeen and the North-east, some older geezers and a large number of families. The journey is not very long from Aberdeen to Gothenburg, so breakfast was the first item on the agenda. Food was not my primary concern as the lack of sleep and the beginnings of a hangover began to kick in, but a couple of fluid ounces of my favourite tipple from a charming stewardess squared me up and I was ready for the rest of what was to be an eventful and historic day.

At Gothenburg airport the fans flooded out with the usual burst of the Northern Lights and was on to our coach to discover we were billeted a good 10 kilometres outside the city.

After booking in to the clean, if a trifle Spartan accommodation, I then had the task of meeting up with Alastair and defining for the last time what our duties would be.

I required to be clean and tidy for that, of course, with the game being in the evening, but a quick check through my changes of underwear revealed I had come without a razor, an essential party of a reporter's equipment in those days before designer stubble was regarded as anything other than the height of slovenliness.

A plea to the hotel staff failed to unearth a razor, but a short distance away was a little general store, where I was able to buy a packet of disposable razors and to set out on my trip to the centre of Gothenburg in pristine condition.

The day had started out fine weatherwise and I came across a fellow scribe after picking up my accreditation for the game and we had a decent lunch on an outdoor restaurant veranda before doing a spot of shopping and , as the afternoon turned into evening, we repaired to a bar within sight of the imposing Ullevi Stadium.

There was, as expected, a huge number of North-east people and Aberdonians in the bar and, unbelievably, one of the lads I met, now living in Gothenburg, turned out to be the son of a leading official of Sunnybank Football Club, one of the city's two football clubs to have won the Scottish Junior Cup.

I just happen to be a member of the club and knew his father well, so some rather baffled Dons fans as well as denizens of Gothenburg were treated to the raucous tones of punters singing "Sunnybank, Sunnybank, Sunnybank" to the tune of "Here we Go, Here we go etc" on the Dons biggest day in their history.

A look outside confirmed the weather had taken a considerable turn for the worse and on approaching the giant Ullevi Stadium water was careening off the structure as if a fire hose was being trained from each promontory. It was lowering, dank weather and a first look inside revealed puddles everywhere. The scene was more Gothic than Swedish, with little indication of the joy to unfold for the 15,000 or so Dons fans huddled inside.

The game itself has been out on video for a quarter of a century, so everyone knows what happened, from Eric Black's early opener, to real Madrid's penalty equaliser and John Hewitt's headed winner from Mark McGee's wonderful cross in the second half of extra-time.

What nobody but those in the box saw was the Scottish Press rise as one as Hewitt's header found the net - with the exception of Alastair Macdonald, who was coolness personified as he noted the goal time. You had to admire his calm under fire as he remained the only British reporter seated at his telephone. I liked that.

Then there was the final act as that free kick whistled past Jim Leighton's left hand post and every Dons fan in the stadium heaved a huge shudder of relief. Then, the final whistle, and I was already running around to the other side of the stadium, guided by stadium staff, to get the quotes for the paper.

The rush was worthwhile as the team were coming upstairs just as I arrived. I caught Doug Rougvie's eye as he ascended a set of stairs and leaned over a little balcony to shake his hand. Such was the power of the big man that he almost pulled me over, flashing that famous gap-tooth grin and venturing the words: "It's magic this, isn't it?" Doug had more or less just put me down when Eric Black suddenly launched himself right into my arms and I carried him around for a few steps as he celebrated what was to be eventually regarded as the finest hour for everybody involved in any way with Aberdeen FC.

The contrast between the managers at the post-match Press could not have been more marked. Fergie was positively bouncing, saying: "I'm absolutely delighted that my team have justified everything we've worked for by winning the Cup Winners' Cup" Fergie admitted he had been worried when Real equalised. and the Dons fell out of the game for 20 minutes, but the half-time break had given him a chance to get things sorted out.

After locating and addressing problems, like Peter Weir playing too deep and Mark McGhee and Eric Black not having a positive enough effect up front, Fergie's unsurprising conclusion was: "I think we proved we were a better side than Real Madrid in the second half an in extra time.

The Dons boss had followed hard on the heels of ashen-faced Real coach Alfredo Di Stefano, who picked out Peter Weir and Gordon Strachan as the top Dons. Typically, Fergie put his slant on things rather than just accept the former football great's take on events.

He said: "I personally don't like to single out individuals but we all know what Strachan and Weir can do. Sometimes, in our domestic games, we don't always get both sides of the park working the way we would like but tonight we got it right. Both wings were well worked by Weir and Strachan and Madrid found it too hot to handle."

A haunted-looking but still courteous Alfredo Di Stefano had earlier said he thought Aberdeen's opening goal could have been offside and said that his players had all agreed that it should have been disallowed.

He said: "The terrible conditions and the state of the pitch affected Real Madrid and we were not prepared for the way the ground cut up and caused our players to tire. But I have to say that Aberdeen did play very well indeed, although I thought that the game would go to penalties.

"In the last 10 minutes we wanted to win the game and perhaps we attacked too much, leaving room for the Aberdeen players at the back. We wanted to win, there was no question of us settling for anything other than a win, but sadly it was not our day and I can only wish Aberdeen the best of luck."

A quick word with Dons chairman Dick Donald, tearful but in no mood to admit it, and it was back round to the press gantry and a marathon telephone session with an Aberdeen Journals copy telephonist specially selected for the job and a treat to work with. Work-wise it was all over.

Back at my hotel there was a post-match soiree in full swing with the ever-present "Northern Lights" taking centre stage. A couple of Dons fans were seen leaving with a couple off astonishingly fit looking Swedish ladies wearing fetchingly flimsy cheesecloth dresses.

I had heard one of the lads asking: "Far's the pairty?" before both headed off into the night clutching a considerable carry-out of spirits and beer in plastic bags. They appeared not to have noticed two giant Swedish males, with slightly dented noses who got in the car with them and the two females.

They were back within 15 minutes, no longer with carry-outs, and one of them was muttering darkly about being conned, though he seemed in no hurry to go back into the night to seek justice.

Next morning it was off to the airport to join the celebrating Dons fans as they jigged and bounced their way on to their flights. My aircraft back to Aberdeen surely mirrored every other one as the singing, celebrating and joy continued, with fans already planning to get another sight of their heroes, either in the parade through the streets of the Granite City or at Pittodrie itself.

For me, it was back to the office to summarise my surprise trip to see history being made by a manager and players set to become legends in the history of a club who will never see anything like it again.

ABERDEEN 2
REAL MADRID 1
SUPER-SUB HEWITT SINKS SPANISH ARMADA

● *Alastair Macdonald's Gothenburg report*

ABERDEEN produced their own version of the scaling of Everest last night, setting the seal on a glorious record setting season by winning the European Cup-Winners' Cup in the rain lashed Ullevi Stadium in Gothenburg.

Substitute John Hewitt, who headed home a Peter Weir cross for a magnificent winning goal in the second half of extra time, was the toast of his native city and the 15,000 Dons fans who flocked to Sweden.

But really this was the greatest triumph yet for the outstanding team-work of the Aberdeen side. The depth of character in the current squad was demonstrated by their never-say-die recovery from the sickening loss of a penalty-kick equaliser after Eric Black had rocked Real Madrid with a sixth minute goal.

Although it took 120 minutes to separate the teams, it was a thoroughly merited victory for Aberdeen against the legendary Madrid club.

Skipper Willie Miller was again a

Extra time goal takes Cup Winners' Cup to Aberdeen

● Doug Rougvie and Willie Miller greet the Dons fans

positive inspiration to his side and other outstanding contributions to the greatest night in Aberdeen Football Club's 80-year history came from John McMaster, Neil Simpson and Peter Weir.

For 20 year-old Hewitt it was an action replay of his substitute appearance against Bayern Munich for he grabbed the goal that beat the Germans.

It was Hewitt's ninth counter in

European competition to make him the most prolific European scorer of the current Pittodrie side.

Aberdeen made a dream start with Eric Black putting them ahead little more than six minutes after the kick-off.

But the Dons suffered a cruel blow eight minutes later when a Alex McLeish pass back, hampered by surface water, left goalkeeper Jim Leighton to take on Real striker Carlos Santillana in a race for the ball.

When the Spanish skipper went flying under Leighton's challenge the referee indicated a penalty, and Juanito levelled the scoring from the spot.

The remainder of the fist half developed into a war of attrition with neither side gaining control but from the outset of the second half the Dons established a grip on the play and came close to settling the issue of several occasions.

A harassed Real defence, however, held out until the 90 minutes were signalled by which time Hewitt had replaced Black injured in an earlier raid.

● Aberdeen get their hands on the prize

berdeen maintained their
periority into extra time and
entually their greater fitness
ntributed to Hewitt's winning
al, which came after a move
tween Peter Weir and Mark
cGhee on the left.

disappointing attendance of
7,804 had to brave deplorable
eather conditions which
reatened to ruin the final utterly
a spectacle.

berdeen supporters who formed
e bulk of the meagre attendance
owever felt that the misery they
dured in torrential rain was all
orth while when that decisive

extra time goal gave Aberdeen a
triumph which only a few
seasons ago would have ben
regarded as being in the realms
of fantasy.

The Italian referee, Gianfranco
Menegali, a martinet by
reputation, obviously made
allowance for the underfoot
conditions in his control of the
game, but he nevertheless
seemed to take an over-lenient
view of some of the Spanish
tackling.

On at least two occasions the
Dons might have been awarded
a penalty but Senor Menegali

just was not interested.

Real's most effective players
were in defence, with Johnny
Metgod in outstanding form,
ably supported by Francisco
Bonet.

The Real attack, however, made
little impression on the Pittodrie
rearguard, with skipper
Santillana in particular having a
lean time.

The heroes of a wet evening
however were the entire
Aberdeen team, who proved once
again that they have the makings
of greatness with a bright future.

BLACK'S EARLY GOAL

ABERDEEN were first to look dangerous when Strachan made a good interception and, although half checked by a Camacho challenge, he got the ball away to Black who transferred it to McGhee on the right. The latter's cross was cleared.

Strachan gave early evidence of his appetite for the game despite the atrocious underfoot conditions, and he initiated several threatening raids in the opening minutes.

It was Strachan who provided the cross which almost brought a dramatic goal in the third minute. Black took the ball on the volley at shoulder height and it crashed off the face of the crossbar with Augustin helpless.

A minute later Simpson forged his way through the surface water, but his parting shot skidded well wide of target.

The ball, which had been changed after Black's shot, again proved unsatisfactory and a third ball was called into play.

Delight for the Dons fans in 6 minutes 34 seconds when the Pittodrie side went ahead.

McLeish moved forward smartly to get his head to a Strachan flag kick and, although the ball was partly blocked by Augustin, it fell at the feet of BLACK, who turned it into the net from close range.

The Spaniards were not too particular about their tackling on the greasy surface and the Italian referee had occasion to warn them

● Eric Black scores the opener

several times.

In 13 minutes a McMaster free kick from just outside the penalty box found Black's head, but the ball skidded well off target.

Real's first raid of any significance brought the Spaniards the equaliser in 14 minutes.

A McLeish passback was slowed down by surface water and when Santillana went down in a clash with Leighton the referee indicated a penalty. JUANITO netted from the spot to give Real an equality which they scarcely deserved at that poin of the game.

The Dons accepted this reverse and redoubled their attacking efforts. McMaster sent Strachan away on the left in 21 minutes, but his fast cross sped out of the reach of any of his attacking team mates.

As the game entered the second half of the first 45 minutes Real began to show more threat in their attacks.

Aberdeen, however, kept the composure and still had a slig edge on pressure. The Dons poli of defending in the opposition half restricted Real to t occasional breakaway.

One of these brought a corner in minutes. Juanito's flag kick w met by Bonet and his head skidded off the head of team-ma Isidro, and went harmlessly out play.

The game had settled into a gri midfield battle, but it w enlivened by two breaks on t right touchline by Rougvie. T second of these saw the full ba get in a promising cross but Bon was in the middle to head clear.

Metgod demonstrated power – b little accuracy – in his shooting 44 minutes when he sent a 40 ya free kick sailing several feet ov Leighton's crossbar.

The second half opened quiet with Aberdeen making one or tw promising but eventually aborti raids.

Miller left his defensive beat to jo in a build up in 51 minutes b again the attack came to nought.

Two minutes later however th Real goal had a let off. A Stracha McGhee-Weir move opened up th Real rearguard. Weir's cross wa deflected into the air off a defend and Strachan's half volley struc Augustin on the knee on the goa line and the ball was scramble clear.

This sharpened the Dons' attackin drive. A twisting header by Blac from Weir's flag kick brought o an acrobatic save from Augusti out the ball refused to bounce kindly for Aberdeen in the resultant goalmouth melee, before the Real keeper finally flopped on top of the ball.

A minute later, however, Weir broke on the left as the Dons piled on the pressure.

In 59 minutes Augustin had to dive full length to hold a 30-yard drive from Cooper.

Three minutes later a brilliant run by Weir on the left touchline saw him sidestep four challenges in succession before getting in a cross which Black, waiting at the far post, mis-headed over the bar. The referee, however, had already blown for offside.

A Strachan run was rudely halted by a scything tackle by Bonet in 71 minutes but the referee contented himself with lecturing the Spanish defender.

Aberdeen may have been experiencing frustration at their failure to push home their territorial advantage.

There was no evidence of desperation as they continued to build up attacks with precision and purpose.

Augustin caused a moment of panic in the Spanish defence in 79 minutes when he tried to punch out a Weir cross and miscued. The keeper recovered in time to flop on the ball before Black could intervene.

The Dons tried their dummy free kick ploy three minutes later but when Strachan eventually did send the free into the box the ball skidded out for a goal kick.

A minute later a Rougvie cross was headed over the bar by Black but the whistle had gone for an infringement by the Aberdeen striker, who had to receive treatment.

Leighton had his first direct save of the second half in 86 minutes when he held a snap shot from Isidro in a Real breakaway.

Aberdeen immediately retaliated with Strachan breaking through but his attempt to chip the ball over the goalkeeper's head saw it go over the bar.

With three minutes of normal time to go Aberdeen substituted Hewitt for Black, who had been limping since his earlier injury.

The referee signalled the end of 90 minutes with the two sides still locked on level terms.

Real started the first period of extra time with San Jose replacing Camacho and it was the Aberdeen goal which first came under threat. Isidro, however, sent a try wide of target two minutes after the restart.

Aberdeen made a strong claim for a penalty in 96 minutes when Cooper and Isidro went down in a heap in the box as they raced to meet a Simpson cross. Both players required attention before play was resumed with a bounce up, the referee having waved away the penalty claims. Aberdeen again might have had a penalty in the 100th minute when McGhee went down under a Bonet challenge on the by-line, but the referee awarded a corner.

Rougvie's header from the

resultant flag kick by Weir had Augustin scrambling along his line to catch the ball just inside his left hand post.

There were understandable signs of leg weariness on both sides as play went into the second half of extra time but Aberdeen looked the livelier side and they sent their supporters into ecstacies of delight when substitute HEWITT gave them the lead in 111 minutes.

Weir started the move with a break on the left before passing to McGhee, who weaved his way into the box to give him a cross which Hewitt met perfectly to score with a diving header.

The only remaining danger to the Aberdeen goal came twp minutes from time when Real were awarded a free kick just outside the penalty box.

The free kick had to be taken twice before the referee was satisfied with the positioning of the Aberdeen wall and thousands of Aberdeen supporters held their breath as Salguero's drive with the second free-kick whistled inches wide of the target.

ABERDEEN – Leighton, Rougvie, McMaster, Cooper, McLeish, Miller, Strachan, Simpson, McGhee, Black (Hewitt), Weir.

REAL MADRID – Augustin, Juan Jose, Camacho (San Jose), Metgod, Bonet, Gallego, Juanito, Angel, Santillana, Steilke, Isidro (Salguero).

Referee – G. Menegali, Italy.

FERGIE'S DELIGHTED

● *By Jim Dolan*

AN ecstatic Aberdeen manager Alex Ferguson bounced into the post-match press conference to pronounce himself "Absolutely delighted that my team have justified everything we've worked for by winning the Cup Winners' Cup."

The Dons boss pointed out that he was a worried man after Real had equalised from the penalty spot.

He said: "For 20 minutes after Real scored we started to fall out of the game and I was very glad to get half-time over so that I could speak to my players.

"At half-time we got things sorted out and Black and McGhee played up front with more impact, making Real play the ball a lot earlier than they wanted to.

"Peter Weir was having a difficult time against San Jose and was playing more like a midfield player than a forward but when he started to push further forward in the second half we took over and Real were in trouble.

"I think we proved we were a better side than Real Madrid in the second half and in extra time."

The Dons boss followed hard on the heels of Real coach Alfredo Di Stefano, who picked out Peter Weir and Gordon Strachan as the top Dons.

● Alex Ferguson and his assistant Archie Knox hold the cup aloft.

Upon learning the Madrid boss had chosen these players as the top Aberdeen competitors, Ferguson said: "I personally don't like to single out individuals but we all know what Strachan and Weir can do.

"Sometimes, in our domestic games, we don't always get both sides of the park working the way we would like but this afternoon we got it right. Both wings were well worked by Weir and Strachan and Madrid found it too hot to handle."

A sad Di Stefano had earlier claimed that he thought Aberdeen's opening goal could have been offside and said that his players had all agreed that it should have been disallowed.

He said: "The terrible conditions and the state of the pitch affected Real Madrid and we were not prepared for the way the ground cut up and caused our players to tire.

"But I have to say that Aberdeen did play very well indeed, although I thought that the game would go to penalties.

"In the last 10 minutes we wanted to win the game and perhaps we attacked too much, leaving room for the Aberdeen players at the back. We wanted to win, there was no question of us settling for anything other than a win, but sadly it was not our day and I can only wish Aberdeen the best of luck."

ABERDEEN 2

REAL MADRID 1

CHAMPAGNE AND ROSES FOR CONQUERING HEROES

DONS SAY IT: FAN-TASTIC!

● *By John Duckers*

THE DONS conquering heroes returned home yesterday to a reception which matches the heights they scaled in Gothenburg's Ullevi Stadium.

It was carnival day as deliriously happy Aberdonians hailed the men who had done the city proud.

At the airport, on the Dons' open-top bus route and at Pittodrie Stadium thousands cheered the players' return.

Work came to a stop, there was mass absence from city schools and they were throwing champagne in Union Street.

And how the Dons enjoyed the big thank-you.

John Hewitt, whose goal clinched Aberdeen's greatest victory, said: "It has been fantastic. These are the best fans anywhere."

Manager Alex Ferguson said: "Magnificent. The whole city has been unbelievable."

For rugged defender Doug Rougvie the reception was summed up in one word: "Brilliant."

● John Hewitt (left) and Eric Black with the trophy

Aberdeen chairman Dick Donald said the club had now established themselves in Europe. "It is a wonderful reception for the boys. This has let people see that Scottish football is very much alive."

Vice-chairman Chris Anderson looked around Pittodrie and said: "There must be 20,000 people here. It reflects how well the team are supported and how well the team have done. This is a wonderful reception – and on a Thursday afternoon too!"

Aberdeen simply went crazy from the moment the Dons

stepped off the plane.

Union Street was turned in single-lane traffic, they we throwing roses, hooting hor and there was even a girl in bikini.

At Pittodrie, many waited mo than three hours to get their fir glimpse of the team.

But what a roar when the eventually arrived shortly befor 5.30pm and strode out holdir aloft the European Cup Winner Cup.

Chants of "champions" rang ou red flags waved and the cheerir was so loud conversation out o the pitch had to be at the top one's voice.

They were there in all ages an sizes from toddlers to pensioner

They had come to enjo themselves … and certainly di that.

It had all been building up fror before 2pm. The ground wa buzzing even then and despit the long wait no one gc impatient. I lost count of th number of times the loudspeake played "European Song" as th

second time, it happened again despite pleas from the players.

Grampian Police chief superintendent John Gordon, who was overseeing crowd control, described the over-exuberance as "disappointing".

He warned: "Boys will be boys. It is like trying to keep quick-silver under control. They were here, there and everywhere. It has happened before and will happen again. There is not a great deal you can do to stop them."

Of the overall police operation, he went on: "It went fairly well bearing in mind it was a very exceptional day in the history of Aberdeen and the football club.

"It was to be expected that there would be some disruption to traffic and life in the city."

For some it was all too much. Ambulances made five calls for people who had either fainted or drunk too much.

The Dons greatest achievement brought messages of congratulations from far and near.

Prime Minister Margaret Thatcher even found time in her election campaign to send a "congratulations and well done" message.

Perhaps she wanted to make sure that manager Alex Ferguson would not take too seriously a banner at Pittodrie yesterday which read "Fergie for PM".

citement grew and grew.

he ground staff and police were ing their best to keep ungsters off the turf but their sk was a hard one.

f they start digging holes in the tch with their shoes Gordon rachan could fall down one," ked one of the Pittodrie staff.

ur supporters ran on to kiss the ntre spot. At one point a tunnel of fans had formed where the players run out but the playing surface was more or less clear for the arrival of the team.

Not for long.

The spectacle was marred by a pitch invasion. The players were engulfed by ecstatic fans and the police had to usher Willie Miller and the cup to safety.

Then, as the Dons appeared a

WHERE WERE YOU?

WHAT were you doing when John F. Kennedy was assassinated? Can you put a place or event to the day when man first walked on the moon or when the Berlin wall crumbled? Where were you when the Dons clinched the European Cup Winners' Cup?

It is one of those landmark occasions for tens of thousands of Aberdeen supporters. Whether in Sweden, on Scottish soil or elsewhere in the world it is a period in time that will never be forgotten for those lucky enough to have lived through it.

The triumph in the Ullevi touched the lives of so many people in so many different ways and for Richard Gordon, now one of the country's best known voices as the anchor of BBC Radio Scotland's respected Sportsound programme, the whole Gothenburg experience provided an emotional rollercoaster ride.

Richard Gordon

Gordon, even in his position of impartiality as a national broadcasting figurehead, has never attempted to hide his club loyalties and his ties to his beloved Aberdeen run deep. He, quite literally, had to beg and borrow to make it to the final against Real Madrid but he is one who can say: 'I was there'.

Gordon said: "I worked in the Clydesdale Bank in Dyce at the time, it wasn't until 1986 that I became involved in broadcasting through hospital radio. Just after the 5-1 win against Waterschei in the semi-final I decided I had to go to the final. After the second leg was completed the plans could be made and I was determined to get onto the St Clair. I had never flown before and was terrified by the prospect, so the ferry was ideal. As it happened all my mates got onto the St Clair but I couldn't get a ticket. I had no option but to book a place on one of the flights, so I've got Gothenburg to thank for starting me flying. I was petrified and it was a nightmare, but it was worth it. I couldn't afford it, but my boss, Ken McLaughlin, was excellent. I ended up with a personal loan for a new fridge and carpets - which paid for the Gothenburg trip."

Gordon was 22 when Aberdeen rocked Real and sent the Spaniards home to think again. Within a few years he had launched his broadcast career in a part-time role, progressing from hospital radio to Northsound before going national with the BBC.

He has travelled the world covering club sides and the national team's exploits but no trip will ever live up to his first, recalling: "I went across on the Tuesday and the abiding memory is of the rain tipping it down. I bought a waterproof jacket and matching

the atmosphere was fantastic with so many Dons fans in the stadium

trousers - which just happened to be red. I must have been a bit of a sight but nothing like that mattered, it was all about the game. The atmosphere was fantastic with so many Dons fans in the stadium, it was the most incredible occasion. I do remember thinking at the time that this just doesn't happen every day, a little team going up against the mighty Real Madrid for a European trophy. I can't help but think it may never happen again. My flight back was on the Thursday, so I missed the main celebrations in the city. On the night of the game I went back to the hotel, had a couple of beers and just lay on the bed soaking in the whole experience."

Gordon's memories of the greatest occasion in Aberdeen's history have been supplemented by the television footage, the new observations blending seamlessly with those cherished first hand views which are as crisp now as they were 25 years ago.

He said: "I remember a free-kick Real had in the last minute of extra-time, the one that they had to re-take. I can still picture the ball flying past the wall and Jim Leighton scrambling across his goal - the ball must have skiffed the post as it went past, but from where we were it took a second or two to be sure it hadn't gone in. When that chance was gone, we really started to feel the team had done it. To see the Aberdeen players running around that pitch after lifting the trophy was just unbelievable. There were some wonderful players but the real strength was the team as a whole and the way Alex Ferguson had put them together, he was a genius in building that side. I did the voiceover for the Aberdeen centenary DVD and it wasn't until I watched back the Gothenburg footage that I realised just how well we played that night and how many chances we created."

For Gordon and the other Dons fans crammed onto the sweeping Ullevi terraces the best of times collided horribly with the worst of times. Amid the drama and celebration there was also a terrible loss, with 22 year-old Philip Goodbrand collapsing and dying during the game.

Gordon said: "The memories are not all happy ones. We watched as a Dons fan was carried from the crowd and it later became clear that he had died. Phil was a former schoolmate of mine at Aberdeen Grammar School and I attended his funeral on my return from Gothenburg. That terrible tragedy is part of the memory for me, whenever I think of that game in 1983 I also think of Phil and his family."

That trip was character building for Gordon in ways he could never have imagined as he set off from Aberdeen and for his fellow passengers in the city's airport departure lounge it would impact in other forms, reaching out an touching them later in life.

Among those who also crossed the tarmac at Dyce to head off on a journey of discovery was a teenage Paul Lawrie. The Aberdonian tasted the highest high as a sportsman in his own right but it was as a schoolboy, far from the fairways of his native north-east, that he first savoured the rush of sporting euphoria that has become part and parcel of his career in top level golf. Lawrie was roared to victory by a passionate Scottish crowd at The Open championship at Carnoustie in 1999 but 16 years earlier the tables were turned as he formed part of the Red Army to cheer on a different type of international sporting success.

The European Tour star made the trek to Gothenburg as a schoolboy and the memories live on.

Paul Lawrie

Lawrie said: "I was 13 when Aberdeen won the European Cup Winners' Cup and I'm proud to say I was there. My father, James, and brother Stephen, who is two years older than me, made the trip to Sweden for the game. My dad is a taxi driver and there were a few of his friends on the same flight. We were on one of the many planes from Aberdeen Airport and spent a couple of days in the city. We were in the middle of Gothenburg and I remember that everywhere you turned, in every coffee shop and every square, there were Dons fans.

"I've been back to Gothenburg a couple of times, playing in the Scandinavian Masters, but never to the Ullevi Stadium. For every Aberdonian, especially those who were there in 1983, the city has a special place in their heart. It was a long time ago but I can still remember the weather, with the rain lashing down on the night of the game. It was a magical night and a magical period for the club."

The Ryder Cup player, who grew up in Kemnay and launched his golf career as an assistant professional at Banchory, lives a jet set lifestyle on the European Tour but has never lost touch with his roots. He still lives in Aberdeen with his Marian and their two sons, who both turn out for a local boys club in the Aberdeen juvenile football league as well as playing junior golf. The family are regulars at Pittodrie and the youngsters have inherited their father's passion for their local team, even if success has been much thinner on the ground during their introduction to the highs and lows of life as Aberdeen fans.

we ended up taking a group of 20 of our managers and staff over for the game

Lawrie said: "As a 13 year-old I probably thought we would win in Europe all the time but as time passes you appreciate how important Gothenburg was more and more. When I went to games in those days the team won by two, three or four goals every week and there were trophies every season so you came to expect that. It has been good to have European football back again and for the family to be able to enjoy the big nights. Craig is 12 and Michael is eight - both of them are mad about the Dons. We get along to as many games as we can, just as I did when I was their age. We were at the Lokomotiv Moscow game, the wonderful victory against Copenhagen. and fantastic draw against Bayern Munich."

Stewart Milne

While Lawrie went on to become one of the city's most decorated sportsmen, the travelling Red Army also included a man who would go on to become Aberdeen's most successful businessman. Stewart Milne was just another fan when he and fellow workers from his fledgling construction company made the trip, not knowing he would later take control of the club he grew up supporting.

The Pittodrie chairman said: "I'm proud to be able to say 'I was there'. We ended up taking a group of 20 of our managers and staff over for the game and it was a wonderful experience. The company had started in 1975 so we were eight years down the road and building up to become a reasonable size, employing quite a few people in the north-east.

"We went over on one of the charter flights from Aberdeen and spent a couple of days in Gothenburg. There was time to soak up the atmosphere around the city and we travelled around quite a bit - I'll always remember hearing the Northern Lights and European Song being sung on every tram you travelled on and every tram that passed. They might have been a bit out of tune, but there was no mistaking them. I don't remember seeing any Spaniards in Gothenburg, everywhere you turned and in every pub you went into there were Dons fans.

"It was my first overseas trip following Aberdeen and I couldn't have picked a better one. I can still picture the game and the goals - but probably not too much of the celebrations that followed! We had a few drinks that night and when we got back to Aberdeen everyone was in a pretty sorry state, although we were back in time for the parade and the amazing scenes on Union Street."

In 2007 Milne sat next to Scotland's First Minister to take in another great night of continental action, this time Pittodrie was the venue as the chairman watched his team trounce Copenhagen 4-0 in the Uefa Cup to earn a place in the last 32 of the competition and guarantee that 2008, the 25th anniversary year, would feature European action at the old ground against old rivals Bayern Munich.

Milne said: "Being involved at the top level in the 25th anniversary season has rekindled the memories and the passions from that period and it has been an exciting time for the club – qualifying for the group stage of the Uefa Cup was great, but to make it through such a difficult pool and into the knockout phase was superb and especially given the milestone that 2008 represents for the club."

The away support in Gothenburg contained a clutch of individuals on their way to fame and fortune in the fields of the media, sport and business to swell the numbers but back home the support for the far flung heroes was even larger. While Gothenburg was over-run by Aberdonians, back in the north-east a whole region ground to a halt to watch history being made.

Diehard Dons supporter Kate Dean is now best known as the leader of Aberdeen City Council but in 1983 she was just starting out in life, one of the thousands who faced the agonising choice of whether to make the trek to Sweden.

Kate Dean

Dean explained: "My husband Brian and I were married in July 82 and had bought an unconverted flat in Woodside. The work needed to make it habitable was done by Brian, who is a plumber and heating engineer, with assistance from friends and family and the minimum of paid-for help. When it came to contemplating the Gothenburg trip, we soon realised that the financial pressures of renovating a flat meant that we could probably have afforded for one of us to go, but not two. In the spirit of young love, we decided that neither of us would make the trip."

And so the future city leader was confined to base, armed with a weapon which until now has been a secret to all but Dean's inner circle - the lucky soup pot. Surely no other piece of kitchenware has ever had a part to play in a football team's European success.

She said: "At that time, I was fairly new to the concept of football, attending Pittodrie infrequenty, along with Brian and my friend Lesley Innes. When the weather got colder, I wimped out from the football and decided to stay home and make a good warming pot of soup for the two of them to come home to. The Dons losing a match was something of a rarity that season - but it seemed to be that if I stayed at home and didn't make soup, then that was the time it happened.

"On the fateful night of the final, we invited another couple to join us at our half-renovated flat to watch the match. Lesley's last words to me as she boarded the bus that would take her by a ridiculously circuitous route to Gothenburg were 'If you can't come with me, you have to make soup!'. The match commenced, as it did in so many living rooms across our fair city, accompanied by one or two small refreshments. From memory, the Dons went one up, and we jumped about like everyone else. Then came the equaliser.

"At that point I started to panic, in case my lack of attendance might be the deciding factor. So, armed with the radio, I headed for the kitchen - and the soup pot. In the grand scheme of soup-making, 30 minutes of extra-time is a long time. When you are superstitiously convinced that the making of the soup is a deciding factor, it's a very long time. I know I started with stock cubes, vegetables and water but as that vital 30 minutes continued, I have no idea what else went into the pot! To my real relief, no-one even attempted to eat the stuff, but to me at the time, the very act of making it was enough. I remember running from the kitchen to the living room when John Hewitt scored, only to be sent back to stir the pot until the final whistle had safely blown. It was an incredible night. I say 'incredible' and mean it - my sons, now 21 and 18, had to be shown the book and the video before they believed it had really happened."

Aberdeen's current Lord Provost Peter Stephen, appointed to the post in 2007, was far from Gothenburg at the time of the cup win but he was still touched by the events unfolding back home – and the souvenir of the era he still cherishes.

Peter Stephen
Lord Provost

Whether near or far, there was no shortage of avenues for absent Aberdeen supporters to keep up to date with the drama and even those forced to miss the game can recall with instant clarity where they were when news of the triumph first filtered through. It was, after all, the moment sporting history was made for Aberdonians everywhere.

Stephen said: "1982 had seen my wife and I returning to our homeland in the north-east following many years in the central belt. We were living in Fraserburgh 1983 and in May of that year were enjoying a French rail holiday which took us to the lovely town of Nice on the south coast. The city was vibrant – full of tourists and atmosphere as the annual film Festival was in full swing during our two weeks there. We saw many famous stars and watched with interest the antics of the paparazzi and local media as they worked."

As Aberdeen stormed to victory in Sweden, the Provost was on the final leg of his own adventure and was in the process of picking up Aberdeen's equivalent to Jose Mourinho's lucky duffle coat.

Stephen exlplained: "Our return journey took us via London's Euston Station. We spent the next 36-hours in the capital visiting most of the tourist attractions, saw the film premier of Duston Hoffman's 'Tootsie' in Leicester Square and also managed a visit to Burberry's ,where my wife and I both purchased a famous Burberry mackintosh. We are both still wearing them, 25 years on. All the newspapers were full of Aberdeen's wonderful victory and it added to the excitement and enjoyment of our holiday - our return home coincided with the bus journey through Aberdeen, which was ablaze with colour and buzz as the players returned in triumph."

That is where the great and good of Aberdeen were on that famous night, but where were you?

ABERDEEN IN EUROPE

ON a cold February night the Pittodrie supporters rose to their feet as their heroes made the mighty Bayern Munich's net bulge. It was not 1983 but 2008 and time for a new generation to sample the big nights on the continental stage.

When first Josh Walker and then Sone Aluko put the Dons ahead against Bayern in the Uefa Cup round of 32 it looked possible a repeat of the famous European Cup Winners' Cup victory was on the cards.

The men from Munich battled back twice to earn a 2-2 draw and completed the job with a 5-1 victory in the return leg in Germany to end an exhilarating run in the competition for Jimmy Calderwood's Aberdeen team.

It turned out to be a fitting 25 anniversary celebration for the Pittodrie club and it had the supporters flocking to the ground which had once been home to the Gothenburg Greats.

Just as lines of supporters snaked around the old ground in 1983 as fans rushed to book their seat for the semi-final and final, the Red Army were once again out in force and fully mobilised.

After disposing of highly fancied Ukrainian outfit Dnipro in the first round the pieces began to fall into place for the silver jubilee. A dream draw in Gothenburg was a bridge too far but instead Aberdeen were handed a nostalgic trip to Madrid, not to face Real but to tackle fierce city rivals Atletico in the group stages of the Uefa Cup.

The Dons have cult status among sections of the fanatical Atletico support, with pictures of the victorious 1983 team hanging in bars in the Spanish capital as a lasting tribute to their giant slaying act against Real in Sweden.

Even 25 years on, the Scottish team was assured of a warm welcome and thousands of fans were ready to take advantage. Early estimates suggested 6,000 would travel to the continent for the Madrid match but, with the hosts riding high in the glittering La Liga, tickets for away followers were limited to 3,000 despite desperate pleas from Pittodrie officials.

The club opted to open the concourse of the Richard Donald Stand to accommodate the growing crowd clamouring for a ticket, with every single one snapped up in an instant.

Even the lack of a guaranteed seat was not enough to deter thousands of Aberdeen supporters from travelling for the biggest game in the club's recent history and eventually Atletico bowed to the weight of public pressure and released seats to accommodate the Scottish visitors.

It was not just the glamour tie in Spain that drew the crowds. A crowd of 18,843 packed into Pittodrie on November 8 for the fixture against Lokomotiv Moscow, just a few thousands short of capacity for European fixtures.

Again fans had queued in their droves to secure a ticket for the occasion as the club savoured its first taste of the group stage of the Uefa Cup.

The passage to the lucrative league phase, which was estimated to have earned close to £1million for the cash strapped Reds, was far from easy. After holding Dnipro 0-0 in the first leg at home Aberdeen scored a shock 1-1 draw, courtesy of a stunning Darren Mackie header with echoes of John Hewitt circa 1983, to squeeze through the first round courtesy of the away goals rule.

It was a pleasant surprise for Calderwood, who is insistent that Dnipro would have been contenders for the Uefa Cup crown had they not been dumped out of the competition by his shock troops.

Head to heads against Panathinaikos of Greece, Russian big spenders Lokomotiv Moscow, Atletico Madrid and Danish outfit Copenhagen were the reward.

All had mass appeal and sent a buzz around the city as European football made a timely return in the season that marked a landmark celebration for the Gothenburg legends.

A 3-0 defeat against Panathinaikos, 1-1 draw against Moscow and 2-0 defeat in Madrid, on a night marred by heavy handed treatment of Dons fans by Spanish police, could not take the shine from the occasions. The game against Copenhagen and stunning 4-0 victory rounded off a group campaign which had reinvigorated the Aberdeen support after a lengthy European absence.

The dream draw against Bayern in the last 32 was the icing on the cake, with in excess of 20,000 crammed into Pittodrie for the home leg and thousands making the trip to Munich for the second tie just a week later.

The imminent anniversary celebrations were not the only factor stoking the passions of the north-east football followers. A European drought was another key factor, with the club returning to the continental scene after an agonising five year absence.

The 2002 run in the Uefa Cup was under the stewardship of enigmatic Danish manager Ebbe Skovdahl. It ended in defeat but not disgrace beneath the sprawling stands of the Olympic Stadium in Berlin after a gallant yet fruitless performance over two legs against Hertha. The first, in Aberdeen, had ended 0-0 and the second in a single goal reverse. The close fought Berlin ties, only settled by a late goal by substitute Michael Preetz, were one of the highlights of Skovdahl's colourful spell at Pittodrie. His curious turn of phrase and unusual approach to the game, which included ordering a mattress for each of his players to enable them to sleep in a darkened players' lounge between training sessions, were only part of the story.

One of the most embarrassing European results in the history of the Dons was another big part of the Skovdahl tale.

That fell in 2000 in the Uefa Cup. Having qualified by virtue of their domestic cup final appearance the previous season, the Dons were paired with Irish side Bohemian in a preliminary round tie. The part-timers stunned the Dons in the first leg and silenced a crowd of 13,638 at Pittodrie with a shock 2-1 victory. An own goal in the return leg on the Emerald Isle handed Aberdeen a hollow 1-0 victory, not enough to prevent them tumbling out of the competition on the away goals rule and falling from grace in unexpected fashion.

No team could ever compete with Sir Alex Ferguson's class of 1983, a peerless side that set a standard never to be matched by the Dons teams which have followed.

Prior to the Bohemians debacle, Roy Aitken had given a glimmer of European hope during a difficult period with his side's exertions in the Uefa Cup in 1996.

Despite a surprise 3-1 defeat against Lithuanian opponents Zalgiris Vilnius in the second leg of the preliminary round that term, a convincing 4-1 win in the first leg thanks to a Billy Dodds double and goals from Duncan Shearer and Stephen Glass earned an away goals win.

Welsh club Barry Town were overcome in the first round, beaten 3-1 in Scotland and held to a 3-3 draw on their own patch. It was hardly the stuff of legend, but at least it was another hurdle negotiated and the form of Dodds, who netted another brace in the draw in Wales, cheered the travelling support.

Brondby halted the 1996 run at the second round stage with a 2-0 first leg win at Pittodrie. The second leg ended goalless.

Going out to the Danes was respectable, especially compared to what had gone before. In 1994 there was more than a hint of irony when a European result began to unravel the Dons career of the man synonomous with the best of Aberdeen's efforts at that level.

As Willie Miller stood in the Pittodrie dug-out on August 23 and watched the team he managed struggle to a 1-1 draw against Latvian underdogs Skonto Riga he must have wished the ground would open up and swallow him whole.

A 0-0 draw in the away leg had appeared far from a disaster but the outcome of the return on Scottish soil was catastrophic. Aberdeen were out of the competition before even getting past the preliminary stage and Miller's coaching career was drawing to a close.

The imperious skipper's other managerial experience of continental competition came in the European Cup Winners' Cup in 1993. On October 20 that year the glory days were in danger of returning, the flashbacks to a decade earlier were in full flow.

Miller led his team out, as manager this time, against top class opposition and, for a spell at least, the Dons dominated.

Torino, sitting pretty in fifth place in the world renowned Serie A, were in danger of being humbled by the men from Pittodrie.

The Turin side included defender Roberto Mussi building up to his appearance for the Italian national team in the 1994 World Cup and Uruguayan striker Enzo Francescoli. Not surprisingly Miller opted for a safety first approach in the opening encounter at the Stadio della Alpi. Duncan Shearer and Scott Booth were both relegated to the bench but it did not hamper Aberdeen's attacking efforts. Mixu Paatelainen put the Scottish side ahead when he headed home from a Paul Kane free-kick. It was a good start but it soon got better. It was 2-0 when Eoin Jess connected with Paatelainen's cross. With two away goals to their credit, Aberdeen appeared to be cruising to a famous victory.

In European competition the Dons had never surrendered a two goal lead by the record books were about to be re-written in unwanted fashion. When Torino defender Sergio pulled a goal back just before the interval it gave the Italians renewed hope. Second half goals from Silenzi, who led the Serie A scoring chart, and Alguilera, courtesy of a deflected free-kick, gave the men from Turin a 3-2 lead to take into the second leg at Pittodrie.

A 1-0 win on home turf would have been enough to take the Dons through and when Lee Richardson opened the scoring the impossible dream came back into sharp focus. The visitors regrouped and a goal in each half took them through 5-3 on aggregate. Arsenal, in the quarter-finals, were the team who halted Torino's push for European honours that season. Eoin Jess scored twice in each of the first round ties against Icelandic side Valur, as the Dons won 3-0 away and 4-0 at home with additional goals from Duncan Shearer in Iceland and Joe Miller and Brian Irvine at home, to set up a mouth watering clash with the Italian stars.

Alex Smith, Miller's predecessor in the Aberdeen manager's office could not get past the second round stage either despite his success in the domestic cups.

His final European campaign was in 1991, when Aberdeen fell to a 3-0 aggregate defeat against BK1903 of Denmark in the first round of the Uefa Cup.

The previous term Smith had steered the club to the second round of the European Cup Winners' Cup with a 2-0 win against Salamina in Greece and 3-0 victory at home to complete the job. Paul Mason and Hans Gillhaus secured the vital away win while Craig Robertson, Eoin Jess and an own goal secured safe passage.

Legia Warsaw proved to be tougher opposition in the next phase and after a 0-0 draw in Scotland the Poles claimed a 1-0 win on their own turf to end the Aberdeen hopes.

Austrian side Rapid Vienna, in 1989, and German outfit Dynamo Dresden one year previously put Smith's side out of the Uefa Cup in the first round as a succession of managers toiled in their efforts to live up to Ferguson's reputation on the big stage.

Ian Porterfield had one attempt and emerged with his reputation intact. He presided over the 1987 Uefa Cup adventure which began with a single goal victory against Bohemian in the first round, Jim Bett doing the damage after a 0-0 draw in Ireland in the first leg, and ended in bitter disappointment in Rotterdam in the second round.

Having defeated Feyenoord at Pittodrie in the home leg courtesy of Willie Falconer and Joe Miller's goals in the 2-1 success, the Dutch side fought back to win 1-0 in the Netherlands and consign Aberdeen to an away goals defeat.

Aberdeen's post-Gothenburg trials and tribulations in Europe have been lacking in glamour. The visit from Feyenoord, the 1970 European Cup winners, in 1987 was one of the exceptions and the Dons rose to the occasion, tackling a side who had won a Dutch league and cup double three years earlier.

The manager drafted in Peter Weir for his first start of the season and he had a part to play in the 2-1 victory. The men from the Netherlands opened the scoring through a Lars Elstrup penalty, after former Rangers striker Dave Mitchell had gone down after colliding with Jim Leighton, but the Dons hit back. First Falconer, settling into his new role at left back, ventured forward to score with a header from Weir's free-kick and then Miller scrambled the ball home for an important home win.

A draw was all Aberdeen needed and they set out in the away leg to frustrate Feyenoord. Ulimately the exercise failed, with the Rotterdam side claiming the 1-0 win which they needed to progress.

It was in fact Ferguson who came closest to repeating the European glory he masterminded. While his final continental campaign with the Dons ended with a 4-2 aggregate loss to Swiss foes Sion in the European Cup Winners' Cup in 1986 there

were other highlights aside from 83.

Those included the European Cup run of 1985/86 which ended in the quarter-finals in Gothenburg, when IFK made it through on away goals after a 0-0 draw in Sweden on the back of their 2-2 stalemate in Aberdeen.

To reach the last eight Ferguson had navigated his way past Icelandic side IA Akranes with 3-1 and 4-1 wins in the first round and then Switzerland's Servette in the second round thanks to a 0-0 draw overseas and 1-0 win through Frank McDougall's goal in the second round.

Aberdeen went into the draw for the quarter-final of the 1986 European Cup with a host of well known names. Barcelona, Juventus and Bayern Munich were all potential opponents but it was written in the stars that the Dons would return to the scene of their greatest triumph.

The tie against IFK Gothenburg presented the opportunity for a

Aberdeen went into the draw for the quarter-final of the 1986 European Cup with some well known names

pilgrimage back to the Ullevi Stadium home of IFK, for the Red Army. Despite the great memories held by the ground, it proved to be an unhappy return for Aberdeen.

The Ullevi was the venue for the second leg and the match ended without a goal, putting the Dons out of the competition following the 2-2 draw at Pittodrie in the first leg. Willie Miller and John Hewitt, Gothenburg veterans, were on target in the first leg but Aberdeen drew a blank in the return tie and returned home to Scotland deflated.

Dinamo Berlin needed a penalty shoot-out victory in 1984 to put Aberdeen out of the same competition. The sides had played out matching 2-1 scorelines as each recorded a home win over the two legs.

The closest brush of all came in the aftermath of the Gothenburg triumph as the heroes came within an ace of defending their crown, reaching the semi-finals of the 1983/84 competition.

The run had begun with a 3-2 aggregate win over IA Akranes and continued with a 4-1 home win over Belgian side Beveren, after a 0-0 in the away leg, in the second round. Hungarians Ujpest Dosza were the unlucky losers in the quarter-finals, winning 2-0 in their own stadium but falling victim to a Mark McGhee hat-trick in the return and bowing out after extra-time.

Standing between the Dons and another final appearance were the Portuguese giants Porto. A 1-0 win in front of 65,000 on home turf gave the continental side a boost going into the tie in Aberdeen and they again ran up a single goal win to end the dream of retaining the cup.

So, with one or two notable exceptions, the post-Gothenburg and Hamburg exertions in Europe have failed to hit the same giddy heights. But then, nothing could ever come close to the exuberance of that groundbreaking season.

When the Ullevi was conquered in 1983 it marked a blockbusting end to Aberdeen Football Club's 12th tour of duty in European competition. The story began in 1967, a golden era for Scottish clubs on the continent on the back of Celtic's win in the European Cup the previous year and Rangers reaching the final of the European Cup Winners' Cup in the same season.

The Dons had Celtic to thank for their own big break, qualifying for the European Cup Winners' Cup despite losing to the Hoops in the 1967 Scottish Cup final by virtue of the Parkhead side's own passage to the European Cup on the back of another title.

The reward for Eddie Turnbull was a first round tie against KR Reykjavik at the start of the 1967/68 season. Should there be trepidation at Pittodrie or fear of the brave new world? No, in a word. The outcome was convincing, with Turnbull's men hammering 10 without reply in front of 14,000 intrigued Dons fans on their home patch. Frank Munro grabbed a hat-trick on a historic day, Frank Storrie bagged a double and Jimmy Smith matched him to add to strikes by Ian Taylor, Tom McMillan and Jens Petersen.

A 4-1 win in Reykjavik took the Dons sailing through to the second round but there was a harsh lesson awaiting against Belgian hot-shots Standard Liege. A 5-0 aggregate defeat sent Aberdeen tumbling out and Turnbull back to the drawing board.

The wily manager had another crack at the new challenge the following term in the Fairs Cup. Slavia Sofia were overcome 2-0 over two legs in the first round but Real Zaragoza came through 5-1 on aggregate to once again halt the Reds at the second round stage.

The next adventure came in the 1970/71 season, again in the European Cup Winners' Cup, and it brought another first for Turnbull and his team. Aberdeen became the first club ever to be knocked out of European competition on penalty kicks after a 4-4 aggregate draw against Honved of Hungary as the result of matching 3-1 wins for each side in their home leg.

That painful experience in Budapest was not the most glitzy tie the club had ever been involved in but higher profile opposition soon loomed on the north-east horizon.

The 1971/72 Uefa Cup, the third continental competition the club had contested up to that point, brought the Spanish stars of Celta Vigo to town for Jimmy Bonthrone's first attempt to get the better of overseas opposition.

His team responded in style with a confidence building 2-0 win at Pittodrie in the first leg of their first round tie as Joe Harper and Jim Forrest combined to shoot down the visitors. Harper scored the only goal of the return game to set-up a dream date with Juventus.

Against the legendary Turin outfit the Dons were beaten but only after a spirited fight. Attempting to turn around a 2-0 deficit from the first leg in Italy, Joe Harper's goal at Pittodrie was enough to earn a 1-1 draw as the Dons fell short of the winning margin required. Once again, the European dream was over before the team could get into their full stride.

Alex Ferguson enjoyed European action in every single one of his seasons in charge

Bonthrone presided over the club's first ever home defeat in Europe when he watched Borussia Monchengladbach edge to a 3-2 Uefa Cup first round win. The Germans completed the job with a 6-3 result in the second leg.

The manager's final Euro service came in the 1973/74 Uefa Cup, guiding the Dons through a 7-2 aggregate triumph against Irish side Finn Harps in the first round as the portfolio of countries visited continued to grow. England was the next stop but, after a 1-1 draw with Tottenham Hotspur in Scotland, a 4-1 loss in London curbed the burning ambition for progress at the top level.

Those 1973 ties were the last on the European stage for four years. In 1977 Billy McNeill became the third Aberdeen manager to try his hand but his attempt was all too brief. A 0-0 draw against RWD Molenbeek in the first round of the Uefa Cup in Belgium was seen as a positive result but a 2-1 defeat at Pittodrie dented that optimism.

Then they began, the Fergie years. Incredibly Alex Ferguson enjoyed European action in every single one of his seasons in charge of the Dons and had plenty of practice before the glory of Gothenburg.

There were highs and lows along the way on the four practice runs which led to the famous 1983 campaign but every experience, good and bad, was part of the learning curve.

In 1978/79 there was success, 5-3 on aggregate, against Marek Dimitrov of Bulgaria before a five goal second round defeat against Fortuna Dusseldorf across two encounters with the Germans.

Opposition from that country proved stubborn for the Dons, who fell 2-1 on aggregate to Frankfurt in the following season's Uefa Cup, in the years ahead.

First there were more valuable lessons closer to home. Ferguson's maturing side eased past Austria Memphis courtesy of a 1-0 home win and 0-0 draw on the continent in the first leg of the European Cup in 1980/81, completing the set of continental competitions for the club.

The mighty Liverpool were more difficult to negotiate at the next stage. The Merseyside men edged out their plucky Scottish hosts 1-0 in the first leg but a 4-0 scoreline at Anfield gave Ferguson an indication of the level he needed to reach to secure the silverware he believed his squad was capable of.

With those lessons tucked away for future reference, the Dons embarked on the 1981/82 Uefa Cup trail with hope and that optimism was not without foundation. Ipswich Town, the holders of the trophy, were formidable first round opponents but there was no fear in the Pittodrie camp. A 1-1 draw at Portman Road, with John Hewitt on target, set up the home leg for a rousing occasion in front of 24,000 fans in the north-east. Peter Weir's double and Gordon Strachan's goal earned a thrilling 3-1 win and sent out a message to the rest of British and European football. The Dons were on the ascendancy.

A 5-2 aggregate win against Arges Pitesti of Romania in the second round teed up another German mission. This time it was SV Hamburg who stood in the path of what was becoming a powerful European machine. Andy Watson, Eric Black and John Hewitt delivered the goods at Pittodrie in a 3-2 first leg win but that slender advantage was not enough. Despite Mark McGhee's goal against his future employers in Germany, the hosts hit three of their own in the second leg and progressed with a 5-4 win.

Ferguson had every reason to be proud of his side's achievements and good cause to be excited about what lay ahead for the Dons. All those hopes and dreams stored up over 15 years of European competition were about to be realised with style, panache and true Scottish grit. The stage was set for the most memorable season of all.

THE BUSINESS OF GOTHENBURG

N November 1983 Aberdeen chairman Dick Donald stood up to address the club's annual meeting. Within 240 seconds he had successfully concluded the business on the agenda, setting a record unlikely every to be beaten.

During the whirlwind meeting he described the era as "the most successful in the 80-year history of the club". The message was simple: the club has money in the bank and has a European trophy in the cabinet. He closed with the line: "Any further questions? No? Then we'll have coffee."

If only it all remained that simple. Since then the game's finances have changed beyond all recognition. Subsequent boards have backed a series of managers with money they could ill-afford and debts have piled up as the success has dried up. As a result, annual meetings became, for a period in the late 1990s and early in the following decade, torturous for directors as they faced a barrage of criticism and loaded questions from angry shareholders.

In the 25th anniversary season of the Gothenburg triumph it is fitting that a sense of financial stability has been restored. The debts, in excess of £10million, remain in place but for the first time in years operating profits are a realistic target. Parallels with 1983 ring true, with the Uefa Cup group stage fixtures in 2007 helping claw back in the region of £900,000 just as the European run under Alex Ferguson had proved so valuable in the 1980s. The ties against Bayern Munich in 2008 doubled the windfall.

In the 1982/83 season turnover smashed through the £1million mark for the first time ever, coming in at just under £1.2million. It led to a profit of £200,000 after tax and kept the club on the steady course plotted so carefully by Dick Donald and his vice-chairman Chris Anderson. For the year up to the end of the 2006/07 season the turnover figure was £7.519million with a £537,000 loss after interest on the club's ever growing debts and other costs were taken into account.

In 1983 the bank balance was boosted by some forward thinking by the Dons and one Aberdeen firm. Years before JVC became the first brand to grace the red jersey of Pittodrie, the name Hydrasun became the first sponsor's tag to adorn the club's kit. The oil and gas company, still going strong in the Granite City, paid the not insignificant sum of £30,000 to have its logo emblazoned on a set of bright yellow tracksuit tops for the squad as they plotted their way through the tournament round by round. Since then sponsorship has developed in huge leaps and bounds, with up to two companies able to endorse a club's shirt while short sponsorship has already been embraced by the Dons.

The early ventures into the corporate world were only part of the 1980s business model, success on the park was the crux. In 1983/84, which included the Super Cup ties against Hamburg which brought in an additional £200,000 in gate receipts and television revenue, turnover leapt up again to £1.9million. Even after a £250,000 investment in keeping Pittodrie at the forefront of football stadia, a profit after tax of £296,000 was recorded on the back of an average attendance in the 1984/85 campaign of 17,000. In the 2006/07 campaign the average gate had fallen by around 5,000 fans.

While Donald spent wisely, he did not shirk his responsibility to his manager and backed Alex Ferguson personally as well as when it came to investment in the Pittodrie squad. The wage bill in the Gothenburg season contained two members of staff earning in excess of £30,000. By the following season that number had climbed to six as the Dons battled to keep their most successful team together.

Total staff costs for 1983/1984 were £914,000 and less than 50% of turnover. For the 2006/07 season the wages to turnover ratio was just over 60%, but that is far from the highest figure that has been recorded in recent times and there are encouraging signs that balance is being restored. The current industry target for that all important ratio is 60% and the Dons were below that watermark in the 2005/06 campaign.

In the summer of 1984, on the back of a European double, the club had £886,000 nestling in its bank account and set aside for a rainy day. It also had a team well placed to dominate the Scottish game.

It was a rare business model in the notoriously volatile football environment. Rangers, struggling desperately to keep pace with the Dons, posted a loss of close to £1million for the 1983/84 campaign. And that was before Graeme Souness arrived to start spending even more wildly.

The Aberdeen accounts for the 1984/85 season did raise some concerns that the Dons were in danger of following Rangers down a dangerous path, with a staggering, at that time at least, annual salary of £120,000 attributed to Alex Ferguson. The chairman moved quickly to allay any fears the fans may have had, insisting the figure was a one off and included settlement of a number of bonus payments and clauses within his contract.

Whatever Ferguson earned, he had more than paid his way. The team which put Real Madrid to the sword in 1983 cost just £320,000 in cash to put together, or £490,000 if you factor in player swaps into the equation. Nine of the 12 players were home grown, with only Gordon Strachan, Mark McGhee and Peter Weir commanding transfer fees.

In turn, as the team naturally began to break up, the same group of players raked in £3.05million when they were sold to clubs in Scotland, England and on the continent. Only Willie Miller, through retirement, Alex McLeish and John McMaster did not pull in a fee when they eventually moved in different directions and every single one of the other nine was involved in a six-figure deal, from the £100,000 paid by Leicester for Peter Weir to the £750,000 it cost Manchester United to purchase Jim Leighton.

That net profit in excess of £2.5million from the sale of the 1983 team helped give the club stability for a number of years and the lucrative transfer markets were a godsend for the Dons, with money reinvested to keep those who stayed on the staff happy and to bolster the squad with new recruits when necessary.

When Gary Smith left Aberdeen in 1996 to join Rennes in France he became the first Dons player to take advantage of the Bosman ruling, denying clubs a fee for out of contract players. It proved to be a crippling blow to Aberdeen, who could no longer rely on fees to balance the books, and one they are only now beginning to recover from. The sale of Russell Anderson for £1million to Sunderland in 2007, the first significant export in recent times, was a major factor in the encouraging financial results posted a few short months after the captain's departure.

Not that the club survive solely on transfers to keep its books in order during the 1980s heyday. It was a commercially savvy organisation, ahead of its time in many ways, and made the best of the opportunities the European success created.

The commercial spin-offs from Gothenburg also extend to the ordinary fan on the street. Dig deep into your cupboard, delve into your attic … that piece of Gothenburg memorabilia might just be worth a pound or two. On internet auction sites material from 1983 remains in constant demand and there is no sign that supply is going to dry up any time soon. Fancy getting your hands on a programme from the Ullevi showdown with Madrid? It won't be easy, one copy up for online auction quckly attracted dozens of bids and shot past the £30 mark. Not quite a lottery win, but in programme terms a healthy return. A signature from Willie Miller or John Hewitt adds kudos to any auction lot, with anything from commemorative coin sets to autographed photographs on offer at any one time. The line in souvenirs has not finished yet though, with Gothenburg t-shirts still in production and in demand.

The most coveted keepsake of all came close to being lost forever. Willie Miller's prized winner's medal was rescued from a life on the scraphead by the quick thinking cup winning skipper. When his wife had a spring clean of cupboards at their home she piled a tower of medal boxes ready for the bin, assuring Miller they were all empty.
He insisted on his own inspection to be on the safe side – and discovered the glistening gold European Cup Winners' Cup medal in a familiar red box among those destined for the rubbish collectors and a treasured piece of Aberdeen's sporting history was saved.

Miller, and his medal, will be the centre of attention in 2008. The 25th anniversary has served to focus minds within the north-east business community and a series of testimonial events have been scheduled, including a glamour game at Pittodrie on July 12 featuring Sir Alex's Manchester United, to mark the occasion and bring some belated rewards to the 1983 squad. The year has, in the words of organisers, been designed to bring closure on the events at the Ullevi as the players seek to look to the future. They can try, but for Dons fans it will be impossible not to continue to hark back to those golden days.

It is not just the Gothenburg players who will be making a comeback. One of the lasting reminders is also in line for a return to prominence is The European Song, the record which became one of the theme tunes to Gothenburg. In 2008 the man behind the track is hoping it could yet be re-released.

Quarter of a century on, songwriter Harry Barry could still have a night out on the back of his contribution to the occasion. The Coatbridge based musician said: "I was up in Shetland recently when somebody pointed out that I had written The European Song - all of a sudden I had people desperate to buy me drinks. Its amazing the fondness people still have for it."

Barry had no link to Aberdeen before he became involved in the 1983 project, joining the Red Army courtesy of his part in another of Scottish football's anthems from that period in the game. He explained: "I had played drums on Ally's Tartan Army and was involved in a football album for the World Cup in 1978. In fact my song Scotland Again, which is still popular, came from that recording. A company called Pro Scot in Glasgow was keen to do something for Aberdeen's run in Europe in 1983 and approached me because they knew I'd been involved in football songs before. I got it written and then spent a week in the studio recording it, they were very happy with the finished product."

And so were the Aberdeen supporters. The European Song sold out in double quick time and demand far outstripped supply, catching the record company by surprise and leading to a missed opportunity. Barry said: "I had a record company of my own and had quoted them to produce the discs but instead it went to England to be manufactured. After the initial run of 55,000 Pro Scot went into liquidation - that was unfortunate because I'm convinced The European Song would have sold far more if extra copies had been available. It exceded all of my expectations. I thought maybe 10,000 or 20,000 records would be sold but every single one of the 55,000 was snapped up and I'm sure it would have been 155,000 if they had been available."

Barry, now in his 60s, is still making records with The Big Elastic Band and is in the process of writing a musical entitled 'When big Roy sang on Annie McGregor's juke box', which charts life in Scotland in the 1950s and 1960s. Intriguingly, he has revealed on the 25th anniversary of Gothenburg than one of the most famous lines in Aberdeen musical history made the record against his better judgement. He said: "The line 'We're gonna do it' was a change from what I had written originally, it was what the company wanted. I felt my version sang a bit better." So what should The European Song have sounded like? That is for Barry to know and the rest of us to guess.

The media also had a captive audience, particularly in the aftermath of the cup final, and quick thinking staff at Aberdeen Journals capitalised by using a Bristow's helicopter to fly bundles of copies of the Press and Journal and the Evening Express to the St Clair as it ferried 500 supporters back from Sweden across the North Sea.

The newspapers which were snapped up onboard the St Clair and back on home soil were packed with iconic images which have stood the test of time. A quarter of a century on, the Aberdeen Journals photo sales department continues to meet substantial demand from fans determined to preserve those precious moments forever. The final whistle sounded long ago, but the business of Gothenburg is still alive and kicking.

THE EUROPEAN DOUBLE

 **A** **BERDEEN'S** victory against Real Madrid sent shockwaves around the football world but the glory of Gothenburg was no flash in the pan. By the end of 1983 the Dons had confirmed they were indeed kings of Europe by defeating SV Hamburg over two legs to claim the European Super Cup title.

Hamburg, who had beaten Juventus 1-0 in the final of the European Cup the previous season, had dumped the Dons out of the Uefa Cup in the 1981/82 season when they came through 6-3 on aggregate.

While the Super Cup gave the Pittodrie side a coveted second continental prize, the road to claiming it was not simple. For one thing, both clubs had heavy commitments domestically and in the traditional European competitions and fitting in two extra dates proved a logistical nightmare for Uefa.

When the dates were eventually set and Aberdeen brushed aside the German challenge there was another unexpected twist. The club discovered that the European Super Cup did not actually exist in anything other than name, instead of a trophy they received a commemorative plaque to parade around Pittodrie on their lap of honour.

Aberdeen District Council sprang into action, writing to Uefa to volunteer the funding to create a fitting cup, while the Dons even offered to dip into their own coffers to foot the bill for a silversmith to create a trophy.

Dick Donald, in his representation to the governing body, said: "The general reaction of our supporters and players was one of astonishment that such a prestigious competition did not have a traditional cup as an award."

Uefa were not happy with the offers of financial support, making it clear that only they could sanction and provide a prize for its own competitions and eventually, after a meeting of its executive committee, made contact with the Aberdeen board to confirm that the club's pleas would be answered the European Super Cup would finally be created.

A 0-0 draw in Germany in the first leg on November 22, 1983, was far from inspired but it was a positive result. Alex Ferguson said: "We played too far back at times instead of in our opponents' half. We're a young side and it showed, but we can play better and I'm satisfied with the result."

It left Aberdeen with it all to do on home turf on December 20, the manager was confident – a sentiment shared by the bookmakers, who made the Dons clear favourites for the title. Alex Ferguson said: "This game is as important as any cup final we have taken part in. This time, though, we have a reputation in Europe and we must try to live up to it."

Hamburg, spearheaded by the talented duo Felix Magath and Manni Kaltz, were a dangerous proposition but were hit by unrest during that period. Strikers Dieter Schatzsneider and Wolfram Wuttke were at the centre of the storm, being accused on not contributing to the team effort. It took a clear the air meeting between players and the management team just hours before kick-off at Pittodrie to settle the team selection for the game against Aberdeen.

For the home side it was far more simple and settled. John McMaster was called in to deputise at left back for the suspended Doug Rougvie while it provided new signing Stewart McKimmie with his first taste of European football. The omens were stacking in favour of the Scottish hopefuls – with the two teams greeted on the Pittodrie turf by the type of driving rain that had characterised their Gothenburg win.

live coverage was broadcast worldwide, from Monaco to Algeria

The masterplan soon fell into place as second half goals from Neil Simpson and Mark McGhee killed off the challenge from the visitors. For Peter Weir it was an extra special evening – as he was getting stripped and preparing helping the Reds to success, a few miles up the road at the Aberdeen Maternity Hospital his son Stuart was born.

After the second leg, Manager Alex Ferguson beamed: "The standard the players reached on Tuesday was magnificent but it is a standard we have come to expect from them."

Aberdeen had cemented their place at Europe's top table in front of a global audience of millions. Live coverage was broadcast worldwide, from Monaco to Algeria and many points in between, while Grampian Television also sold highlights to Thailand, Malaysia, Singapore, Brunei, Hong Kong, Pakistan and Malta.

HOW THE TEAM BROKE UP

JUST as a succession of Aberdeen managers had a hand in building the team which swept European opposition aside with such confidence and ease in 1983, a series of men also had a hand in dismantling the greatest side in the history of the Pittodrie club.

Alex Ferguson, Ian Porterfield, Alex Smith and Willie Miller all presided over the transfers which bit by bit removed the bricks which had formed such a solid unit. Some transfers were unexpected, some were unwanted by the club and others were actively encouraged by the coaches who faced the ominous task of trying to recreate the glories of that famous summer.

Even the mighty Sir Alex was powerless to stop the early stages of erosion which threatened his Dons empire. The first to be washed away, just a year after the tide of euphoria which had swept the city, was Mark McGhee.

As McGhee approached the end of his Pittodrie contract at the close of the 1983/84 season he had attractive options to consider. Aberdeen had made him an offer to stay while he was also provoking interest from the continent, with German clubs particularly keen.

Bayer Uerdingen, backed by a major pharmaceutical company, led the pack but in the end they could not compete with SV Hamburg. McGhee departed for Germany, where he received a large salary and perks including Mercedes club cars.

Ferguson insisted the loss of the Scotland star was a valuable lesson and said: "The problem was the big gap in time between negotiations – and that won't be allowed to occur again. The players were not keen to talk to me during the season about new contracts and I know now we made a mistake by waiting only a year before their contracts were up.

"It was easy for some of them to get carried away after last year's success in Gothenburg and they became harder to deal with. I started talking to Mark about staying in August and I was waiting for him to come back with a realistic view of the situation – but he only came back to say he was leaving."

McGhee signed off with an extra-time winner against Celtic in the 1984 Scottish Cup final before clinching his £300,000 transfer. He had impressed in the European Super Cup triumph against Hamburg, scoring against the Germans, and was recruited to join a side who had just missed out on the chance to land their third successive league title and had surrendered their European Cup crown.

there is no way I could have played for another Scottish club after such a successful time at Aberdeen

McGhee, 26 when he moved to the Bundesliga, said: "There is no way I could have played for another Scottish club after such a successful time at Aberdeen. The only English sides I would even have considered are Manchester United and Liverpool and the challenge of playing for Hamburg attracts me."

The summer of 1984 saw two members of the Gothenburg team depart Pittodrie for what they hoped would be greener pastures. Certainly the moves were financially beneficial, although neither player would enjoy the type of playing success which had become par for the course with the Dons. Doug Rougvie was the second player to leave, although he did stay closer to home than McGhee by opting to remain in Britain and taking what would become a well trodden path to English football as the legends of 1983 discovered their continental exploits had extended their reputations beyond the normal confines of Scotland.

Rougvie had been the subject of a £250,000 bid by Middlesborough, managed by Scotsman Bobby Murdoch, during the summer of 1981. The offer was rejected by the Dons, who saw the defender as a vital cog in the defensive machine Alex Ferguson had painstakingly constructed.

Ferguson said at that stage: "There is no way Rougvie is going to be transferred to Middlesborough or any other club for that matter. The big man is enthusiastic and powerful with plenty of pace and can play virtually anywhere in the side. I need him as a valuable member of my squad. We don't need Middlesborough's money – we are looking to build a side here, not to sell players."

Rougvie, who had feared for his chances of playing regularly at Aberdeen, admitted he had been interest by Boro's approach and eventually he acted on the urge to perform in England. In July 1984 the Red Army was rocked when a man they had elevated to cult status confirmed he was leaving to join Chelsea.

It was not only the fans who were surprised. Manager Ferguson said: "I am very disappointed to be told that Doug has joined Chelsea. I spoke to him at the ground on

Monday and he told me he'd had a very good financial offer from Chelsea – better than we had offered. I told him that I would have to go back and see the board of directors but that was the last I saw of him. He has never come back to see me, and now I learn from the press that he has signed for Chelsea."

The defender was out of contract and agreed a four year deal with the Blues. The clubs later settled on a £250,000 fee for a player who had been capped by his country and tasted European success.

Rougvie said: "After 12 years at Pitodrie it was obviously a difficult decision to leave. I have built up a good relationship with the fans and will miss them, but I've got my own life to lead and I am positive I have made the correct decision. As for Aberdeen, the terms were not acceptable. It's as simple as that and we decided it was time to make a move."

Ferguson never attempted to hide his displeasure when he lost players who he considered should not be leaving. There were few exceptions, but Neale Cooper proved to be one. Cooper was a true protégé of the manager and there was sympathy rather than dismay when he eventually decided to call time on his days as a Dons star, having tortured himself over a period of more than a year after becoming disillusioned with life in the goldfish bowl of Scottish football. The very qualities which made Cooper a favourite with Aberdeen fans eventually drove him to seek a new club.

His career reached a crossroads in the summer of 1985, when he rejected the offer of a new contract. He was left out of the club's pre-season trip to Switzerland because of his failure to commit, having only penned a one year deal the previous season.

Ferguson said: "We can't twist his arm into resigning. Naturally we hope he stays with us. We have made him an offer and it is now up to Neale."

Eventually he did sign on, but significantly he agreed to only another 12-month contract. Money was not the issue for Cooper, instead he was unsettled by the treatment he was receiving from opposition fans who targeted him because of his combative style. He also admitted concerns about his reputation amongst Scottish referees.

By the close season in 1986 those concerns had not diminished and he said "I am a marked man in the Premier Division. I was booked nine times in the past season and the manager and myself have spoken about it – we reckon only three were legitimate. I have to say the situation is becoming impossible for me and I feel I have to move away. Scottish clubs have made approaches for me but I would never leave Aberdeen for another Scots club. It would be pointless anyway, because I doubt if the attitude of referees would change."

Sheffield Wednesday, under Howard Wilkinson, were keen along with Chelsea but it was Aston Villa who won the race for the 22 year-old. On June 22 1986 he made his decision. Cooper said: "I will be going to Aston Villa – but this is a really sad day for me. I have been with Aberdeen since the age of 10. I feel I would be welcome back back at Pittodrie at any time and that is the only way I wanted to go from Aberdeen. The club and the manager have been very good to me."

The pain of departing his first football love was offset by the excitement of his new adventure. Cooper added: "Villa are a big club who are going places. Their stadium and training facilities really impressed me. In fact, when I walked into Villa Park I thought it was out of this world. I can only liken it to looking for a new house – you come across one which you know instantly is for you. There were a number of factors in my decision, including an indication by Graham Taylor that he intended playing me in my favourite position as a central defender."

Ferguson said: "Neale has ben one of our most important players and his leaving is a big loss for us. He has, however, been completely honest and open in all his dealings with us and we can only wish him all the best for the future."

The Dons wanted £500,000 to compensate for the departure of such an influential player but could not agree a fee with the English side, who wanted to pay £200,000. A tribunal set the price at £350,000 and the deal was done.

A player who left on less favourable terms was Eric Black, who decided that continental football was the way forward for him. It was as the summer of 1986 approached that he decided to make the leap from the club which had given him his finest hour. At the time his transfer was revolutionary in a sense and it created a storm of media interest, whipped up in part by Ferguson as he did his best to keep the core of his side together at Pittodrie but must have known he was fighting a losing battle with some of his star players.

Black had used an agent to broker his 1986 transfer, a rare course of action for a Scottish player in the 1980s. It sparked heated debate and Harry Lawrie, secretary of the Scottish Players Union, hit out: "We sent players a circular last year telling them to keep away from agents. These guys can take anything from 20 to 25 per cent of a transfer fee – but it doesn't always stop there. Once a player starts earning bonuses and sponsorship cash, the agent gets his cut of that too."

The furore surrounding Black's use of an agent illustrates just how much football has changed in the post-Gothenburg days. Now a player is the exception if he does not employ a representative – in Alex Ferguson's era they were banned from stepping foot inside Pittodrie. The manager had his say, claiming: "Eric Black has been badly advised.

I think he was a bit concerned that no British club had come for him. Now he has gone to an insignificant club in Europe. His agent has done him no favours at all. He could have done much better for himself if he had only waited until the end of the season and then used the close season to find a club more suited to his talent.

"From time to time you get players who believe the grass is always greener elsewhere, but once they are away they always turn and say what a great club Aberdeen are. We can do without this, because if we are such a great club why do they want to go? It is up to us to try to make Aberdeen an attractive club to stay with. We can't stop players going under freedom of contract. I wouldn't mind so much if it were done openly and with consideration given to the club."

Ferguson's anger stemmed from Black's decision to commit to Metz while still under contract at Pittodrie, although his deal was due to expire it was not common practice to begin negotiations until the actual date had passed in those pre-Bosman days. The manager's response was immediate and he dropped Black from the 1986 Scottish Cup final when news of the impending move broke.

The fee was decided by Uefa, who had a formula which awarded clubs 10 times a player's salary as compensation for their loss. It netted the Dons £350,000 in 1986.

He proved good value for money, going on to lead the French scoring chart in his first season with eight goals in his first eight matches. He was rewarded with a five year contract by his ambitious new club and catapulted himself into the Scotland reckoning. Metz had won the French national cup two years prior to recruiting Black and, despite a limited track record, were keen to build on that success. Black said: "When I met the president and manager, I was impressed by their ambition to be successful.

They seemed geared to do well and, having tasted success with Aberdeen, I was interested in maintaining that success.

"I could not have wished for a better club than Aberdeen with which to start my professional football career and I have thoroughly enjoyed my spell at Pittodrie – but I felt the time had come to think of my future security. It's just a pity the story leaked out when it did."

Black was just 22 when he flew in to start a new life in France and he embraced the culture with both hands, helped by the fact his wife Nina had family just across the border in Germany.

Gordon Strachan was another Dons player with continental options but he chose to follow the path of Rougvie and Cooper south of the border in August 1986, when he became the fifth member of the Gothenburg dream team to part company with the club as he attempted to keep his passion for the game burning bright. His manager was not amused with the manner in which the decision was announced but Ferguson would later follow in the Scotland international's steps by making the move to Manchester United.

Strachan broke the news of his plans to head for fresh pastures in an interview with the Evening Express. He said: "It's not a question of money – it's good at Pittodrie – but a change of scenery is essential to my career. I would be lying if I said I didn't want to see what other countries have to offer. I want to leave Scotland because it gets to the stage where playing at places like Firhill and Cappielow twice a season becomes a bit much. I've tasted all the pies there, met all the tea ladies, and I'd like to meet some new challenges. I don't see how my game can get any better up here and it could well get worse. Obviously England interests me and I would have no objections about going to Spain or Italy."

And so the bidding war began, eventually Cologne and Verona were the two clubs left in the auction. Both thought they had won, with the midfielder signing an agreement with Cologne stating that if he moved to Germany it would be to join them and a similar one with Verona ensuring they would be the only Italian club to secure his services.

Then Ron Atkinson emerged and snatched the prized lot with a £500,000 bid. Strachan said at the time: "I almost went to Cologne. Their officials were superb and I was really keen to join the club – but the chance of joining Manchester United, the greatest club in the world, proved too much. If I'd decided not to go to Old Trafford I might have regretted it for the rest of my life."

Cologne were furious and lodged a complain with Uefa. The outcome was that Aberdeen had to pay the Germans compensation and Manchester United made a similar contribution in the shape of an agreement to play a friendly match against the continental side.

Ferguson, typically, was not happy to part with a player he considered was making the wrong career choice. The manager said: "A club is always sorry to lose a good player but in Gordon's case we have known for two years that he was likely to move on at the end of his contract and provision was made with the signing of Billy Stark last summer. Why players would want to leave a successful club I cannot understand, but if any player does not want to play for Aberdeen, we don't want him. Willie Miller and Alex McLeish have indicated that they want to stay at Pittodrie and I will do everything in my power to accommodate them – but in some cases I just don't know what players want because they have not made their wishes known to me. They know where my office is."

Strachan proved to be the final Gothenburg player to exit during Ferguson's tenure. It was Ian Porterfield who was in charge by the time the sixth Gothenburg great left the building and it was John McMaster who completed the half dozen. McMaster, like Cooper before him, left with the full blessing of everyone at the club and left with plaudits ringing in his ears – in fact, he even continued to train with the Dons after signing for Morton in February 1987 until he had completed his relocation to the west coast. He was 32 at the time and had enjoyed 15 glorious years with the Dons. Porterfield said: "I told John I was prepared to release him to allow him to continue his football career with another club. He has been a good servant to Aberdeen and received his testimonial award as a result. John appreciated that his long term future would not be at Pittodrie and we agreed that he could go down and have talks with Morton in the hope that he could get himself fixed up. I am pleased that things have gone well for him and can only with him the best for the future."

McMaster decided to drop down a league to play in the First Division, taking on coaching duties under Alan McGraw and Jackie McNamara senior at Cappielow before eventually becoming assistant manager. He said: "I didn't want to sell myself short by playing in reserve football at Aberdeen. I always felt I had first team football left in me. I know it's a First Division stage with Morton for the moment, but it's first team stuff." There was close to a year of stability for the remaining members of the class of 1983 before Peter Weir became the next to move on. Weir was sold by Porterfield, having discovered he had a determined fan within the English club scene. At one stage the winger had expressed a desire to see out his playing days with the Dons but the decision was not his to make and he could only stay if there was a genuine role for him to play.

Weir grew frustrated with the lack of first team opportunities following Alex Ferguson's departure for Manchester United and asked for a transfer in 1987. He later withdrew that request but in January 1988, following his recovery from an Achilles tendon injury, interest from Leicester City prompted him to look again at his future. He said: "I feel I need a change. Since recovering from my injury I've been working hard on my fitness, training twice a day in the past week, but reserve football is no good for me and there does not seem any immediate prospect of getting back into the Aberdeen first team. I have thoroughly enjoyed my time at Pittodrie, but I think it is time for a move."

Weir was 29 when he moved in a £100,000 deal, signing a three and a half year contract with the Foxes. Leicester manager David Pleat had been an admirer of the winger's when he was in charge at Tottenham and stepped up his interest after taking charge of the Midlands outfit.

Dons manager Porterfield said: "Peter has been a superb servant to Aberdeen. He came to see me a few weeks ago and said that, because he was in the reserve team and had been suffering a bit of injury trouble, he felt a move would be to his benefit. I knew David Pleat was interested in him and we reduced our price because of Peter's great service."

Leicester felt they had landed a real bargain when they unveiled a two-time European title winning player at Filbert Street. Pleat said: "I am delighted to have signed Peter. He is an experienced player with a lot of skill who has played at the highest level. He is the sort of player you can give the ball to and relax."

Another player coveted in England was goalkeeper Jim Leighton. The Scotland stalwart was one of the safest pairs of hands in the business and nobody knew that better than his old boss Ferguson, who was the most determined member of the pack lining up to chase the Aberdeen legend. He was a valuable asset and his new club had to pay top dollar in the face of strong competition from all corners of the land and beyond. While clubs approached Leighton in hope, there was only one which could have any real confidence that he would commit.

The announcement that the keeper was departing for Manchester United was not made until he had played the final game of the contract which ran to the end of the 1987/88 season but the move surprised nobody in football. While Tottenham as well as French and German clubs had expressed an interest, the opportunity to move to Old Trafford and follow his old manager south was irresistible.

The £750,000 transfer went through in May 1988 but the seed had been sown two years previously, when Leighton starred for Scotland in the 1986 World Cup finals in Mexico.

Speaking after clinching his United ticket, he said: "I needed a new challenge because after the highs of Mexico the following two years were a slog and a lean time for me personally. I found it hard to motivate myself, even under Alex Ferguson and before Ian Porterfield took over. My mind was made up. At one point I was linked with more clubs than I knew there were in Europe – so it was a weight off my shoulders when I was eventually able to turn round and tell everyone I was going to Manchester United.

"I had always hoped to play for them. Ian Porterfield called to say Aberdeen had accepted United's offer and shortly afterwards Alex Ferguson phoned. Within about 10 seconds arrangements were made for me to fly to Manchester. Genuine interest had been expressed by foreign clubs and the money on offer was unbelievable. I know I could have made lots more cash in going to the continent, but the minute Manchester

United came in, money was forgotten."

Leighton had adhered to what had become something of an unwritten rule when he departed for a club outside of Scotland. No Gothenburg player had felt comfortable about the prospect of leaving Aberdeen behind for a rival Scottish team but by the time John Hewitt was allowed to move on the time lapse had eased any nagging fears that existed. Not that Hewitt ever had a reason to worry, regardless of what route he had taken there was never a danger of any negativity towards the scorer of the city's favourite goal.

He broke the mould and opted to stay in Scotland and in April 1989, after a decade's service, news broke that the Gothenburg hero was being allowed to leave his spiritual home. Manager Alex Smith said: "John is perfectly capable of becoming a quality player

my best season was when I played alongside Mark McGhee

and he has indicated to me he needs a fresh start. He also prefers playing through the middle while we feel he's best wide, whether on the left or right.

"We already have players like Charlie Nicholas, Paul Wright and Willem van der Ark who play through the middle while young players like Eoin Jess, Scott Booth, Andy McLeod and John Dickson are also in that category and some of them have been showing signs of needing to progress."

Hewitt, who was targeted by Celtic as well as Queens Park Rangers, Leicester City and Middlesbrough, was determined to carve out a career as a centre forward and at the age of 26 realised he would have to do it elsewhere.

He said: "I signed on again for Aberdeen just before Alex Ferguson went to Manchester United. When he was here he played me through the middle and I feel that's my best position as I'm quick and can score. Ian Porterfield tried to play me as a wide midfielder – but that didn't suit me. My best season was when I was playing alongside Mark McGhee through the middle."

Celtic offered £225,000 and the bid was accepted, although the regular attacking berth Hewitt craved was difficult to secure at Parkhead as he was deployed on the left wing before heading for St Mirren.

Neil Simpson also ended up playing for another Scottish club but his route was less direct than that of Hewitt. More than seven years had passed since Gothenburg when he left Pittodrie but the stock of that cherished crop was still high on both sides of Hadrian's Wall as Aberdeen continued to hold their own among Scotland's leading club sides. He was another who was granted his move by Alex Smith as the evolution of the club continued and plans for a fresh push for honours were formulated by the latest management team, a blueprint which had less and less space for the heroes of the Ullevi.

Simpson's move to Newcastle went through on July 18 1990, with a fee in the region of £180,000 agreed between the two clubs. Magpies manager Jim Smith wanted to make it a double deal but his efforts to add Alex McLeish to his squad were fruitless.

Vice-chairman Ian Donald admitted: "We would probably have wanted more for Neil, who is an excellent player and a decent lad, but for his recent injury problems. I hope the change of club will see him come back as the kind of player who served us so well in the past and everybody here wishes him well."

Manager Alex Smith expressed similar sentiments. Injury had disrupted his final seasons at Pittodrie as well as the controversy surrounding the challenge which led to the injury to Rangers rival Ian Durrant and the subsequent court case surrounding the incident. The switch to England presented a clean slate for Simpson and a fresh challenge.

The move came a year after he had initially asked for a transfer. His request was granted in 1989 but Simpson had second thoughts and opted to stay with his beloved Dons for another season.

A proposed £350,000 switch to Greek side Panathinaikos fell through in 1989 and Ipswich also failed in efforts to recruit him. In 1990 Simpson finally broke away from his home city team, impressed by Newcastle before he had even set foot inside the Tyneside stadium. He said: "I was very impressed with my first look at the ground. Even the main entrance is awesome and playing in front of 38,000 crowds holds a big attraction. Roy Aitken and Mark McGhee have said a lot of good things about Newcastle."

Willie Miller was the only player who saw his playing career with the club draw to an end without an influence from a manager or any personal whim. Mother nature was the deciding factor for the skipper, who had battled against a knee injury in the latter stages of his playing career. Miller was never a player who conceded defeat but when it came to prolonging his life on the pitch he was forced to do just that, with his final outing coming in 1990 at Hampden against Queen's Park in the League Cup. It hastened the veteran defender's entrance to the world of coaching, beginning what proved to be his grooming for a fast-track to the Pittodrie manager's chair when he replaced Alex Smith in 1992.

Miller, in his capacity as team boss, had the role of putting the lid on the Gothenburg team once and for all. He was the manager who sanctioned the transfer of the last man standing, Alex McLeish. Miller and the club did what was right when they opened the door for McLeish to pursue his management dream, perhaps not envisaging exactly how far he would go in that line of work. There was no great fanfare or ceremony when McLeish walked out of the main door, just a quiet sense of mourning for the supporters who had been with the team every step of the way in 1983.

McLeish, who had become captain marvel following Miller's retirement, was a huge loss for the Dons. As the 1993/94 campaign drew to a close manager Miller said: "Alex is having one of his most impressive seasons. He has been offered another playing contract and I'm hopeful he will find it favourable." The terms were not an issue, there was far greater

the Dons fans have always been great to me

incentive offer elsewhere – a managerial breakthrough. Rumours of a move to mega rich Japanese outfit Grampus Eight failed to materialise but talk of Motherwell's interest in making him their boss proved accurate. He was appointed at Fir Park in July 1994 to bring to an end a glittering 18 year career with his first club. He followed in the footsteps of Tommy McLean but also agreed to take on playing duties in Lanarkshire.

McLeish said: "It was only after much deliberation and much discussion with family and friends that I decided to take the job. It will be a big wrench to leave Aberdeen, where I have had so many great times and have watched my family grow. The Dons fans have always been great to me and I just know I will miss them after all these years. I realise I can't go on playing forever and I simply grabbed this chance. It was too good an offer to turn down."

The Dons boss was on hand to pass on his early experiences of management to his former playing colleague. Miller said: "Alex leaves Pittodrie on the best of terms and with the club's complete blessing. If he's looking for someone to talk to about anything at all he knows where to reach me – and there are plenty of former Dons players and managers who would say the same. The first three months of management are the hardest but Alex has all the qualities to be successful."

And so the book closed on the Aberdeen team's Gothenburg heroes. The boots, before long, were all pegged up one last time and the heroes of 1983 set about their new careers, inside and outside the game, with familiar vigour. The big question is if, not necessarily when, we will see their likes again.

THE FUTURE

OLDER, wiser and more realistic – four words to describe captain fantastic Willie Miller 25 years after the event which defined his career at the top level. When the Glaswegian lifted the coveted European prize above his head in 1983 he was driven by the determination to make the Dons the best in the business and he feared no team which dared to stand in his path.

Fast forward to 2008 and, in his role as director of football, the realisation that the game has changed beyond all recognition has forced Miller to temper his burning ambition for success with the only club he has ever served. For Aberdeen, and the man referred to affectionately as 'The Legend' by manager Jimmy Calderwood, the aim first and foremost is to compete with Europe's big guns rather than to swat them aside in the style of Sir Alex Ferguson's famous side.

Miller went through the cathartic process of poring over the good old days during the compilation of his biography The Don in 2007. The book's launch coincided with the fervent reaction to the club's reintroduction to the continental game in the 2007/08 season but while the fans soared high, lifted by the wind of expectation, there was no danger of the board being swept along. While the increased revenue the group games created was welcome, there was no rush to spend the money to repeat the exercise and European football is now being treated as a bonus rather than a divine right. All change from Miller's playing heyday but a pragmatic approach which is beginning to bear fruit. Whisper it, but the future is all of a sudden looking very bright.

Miller admits: "The legacy of the team I played in during the 1980s has made it more difficult for Jimmy Calderwood and the current team. When I came back to the club there was a huge job in restructuring and giving the club its standing in the game back. That is what Jimmy has done – the players can take a lot of credit for what has been achieved. The work Jimmy Calderwood has done, getting back into Europe and to the group stages of the Uefa Cup was a fantastic achievement. To then make it through to the last 32 was very significant indeed, especially given the manner of the 4-0 victory against Copenhagen in front of a full house at Pittodrie to do that."

He faces a battle to persuade the Pittodrie faithful that simply being on the big stage is enough. For a set of supporters brought up on success after success it is a message at odds with the heritage of their team but the director of football is convinced the education process is well under way and that patience is building as the Dons plot their way through the minefield of modern football.

Miller said: "It is a little bit hard to take sometimes when the team is booed off the park because they have only drawn against Falkirk as they were after the first Uefa Cup group tie against Panathinaikos – when you look at Rangers, with their resources, they came back from European ties and were beaten twice in the league at the same stage of the season. We have a way to go to convince the fans that there is something special happening at the club - but we know it and Jimmy knows it."

In fact, the special thing that Miller is aiming for is not entirely new. He's gone back in time for the solution to the club's woes, aiming to recreate the renowned youth policy which gave him his big break in football along with so many of the Gothenburg team. The difference now is that the club is not seeking to rear its own players through choice but due to necessity, the pressure on Miller and his new look youth development team has never been greater. He delved back to the 1980s to lure youth academy director Lenny Taylor to the club, a man who was so influential on the careers of the likes of Neil Simpson during his previous stint working with the Dons youngsters, and wants to restore the 80s ethic.

Miller said: "The youth structure is there to produce our own players and we are doing that. If you look at the resources we have and the fact we go into every campaign with a very tight pool, which gets stretched to the limit, it means we sometimes have to put young players into hostile environments."

The team which took to the field in Athens for Aberdeen's first ever European group game in 2007 against Panathinaikos contained six players who came through the ranks at Pittodrie at various stages in recent years. Michael Hart, Derek Young and Chris Clark were relative veterans while Zander Diamond, Richard Foster and Andrew Considine represented a fresher batch of youth products. The aim for the Dons is to increase that presence in the first team while continuing to progress by bringing established talent to the north-east to ensure European football is a regular occurrence.

Miller said: "When you have a manager who is tactically aware and has done the job that he has done, then I think we have brought back the pride we expect. The results he has had in the league programme over the last few years and the qualification for Europe, tells its own story. Rangers and Celtic are not making claims about winning

European titles, and they are clubs with huge resources. They wouldn't be silly enough to predict that and I'm not a silly person, so I won't go down that road either. Instead I would say tha what we have achieved at the club in a short period of time is huge, giving ourselves four games in the group stage and competing well against the quality of opposition of Panithinaikos, Lokomotiv Moscow, Atletico Madrid and Copenhagen is magnificent and making it through the pool to face Bayern Munich was an even bigger achievement."

It is not just the fans that Miller has to convince about the realistic aims for the Dons in the current climate - the director has to try and keep a lid on his manager's expectations too. Calderwood has been one of his team's fiercest critics during his quest to bring the good times back to Aberdeen but the pressure is self-imposed rather than filtering down from the board room.

Miller said: "We relish where we are and have to realise can only compete as well as we can. Sometimes Jimmy takes it a little bit too hard — but I've been through it as a player and a manager, I know how hard it is to come back from a European tie and produce a performance and get a result in a domestic situation.

"It took the Gothenburg team a long time to get to that position, it wasn't our first experience in Europe as it is for the majority of the players in the current team. The team that won in Gothenburg was built over a number of years and competed against top sides together for two or three seasons before beating Real Madrid. The belief grew as we beat the likes of Bayern Munich. That type of confidence is an important part of any team's make-up.

"You always hope to do well but have to remember we are now only novices in European football. There is a long way to go before we can expect to be playing at this level year in and year out. That only comes with hard work and ability and the challenge is to keep our most talented players at the club. I think it has been a good learning process and if they can get into this position again then the experience of this season will stand them in good stead. Playing at the top level gives a club a certain feeling, a certain buzz, but I've been around long enough to know that success can disappear just as quickly as it arrived. We have had a taste this season of the big occasions and everyone is desperate to continue the progress."

Miller's opinions still count, both within and outside Pittodrie, and the passage of time has reiterated his belief that success is not down to individuals. He is keen to strengthen the bonds which knit the club together, drawing on his own experiences as a player, manager and now director of Aberdeen.

He said: "It is always nice to look back and think about what you've achieved – and to think about the bad times as well, there have been one or two of those to cope with. There have been a lot of people there to help me, people I have worked with: the managers, the coaches, the directors, the fans, the players I've played with and against. Every one was important."

The benefit of that experience is now on tap for Calderwood, although Miller's role is very much hands-off as far as the first team is concerned. While his position does include the delicate responsibility for transfer and contract negotiations, recruitment is very much the manager's domain. Miller's door is always open for Calderwood but his past achievements are as much of a motivation as any advice which is on offer.

The part the Gothenburg greats have to play in the future of the club is a matter which has been debated time and time again, from the day Alex Ferguson departed for Old Trafford to signal a new era on Pittodrie Street. Should the Ullevi troopers forever be celebrated or is the glorious past responsible for heaping unbearable pressure on every player who has graced the turf since 1983? It is something the present manager, watched over in the media room and players' lounge by images of the 1980s team, has given plenty of thought to.

The coach has come up with a clear conclusion, with Calderwood claiming: "I have often heard it said at Pittodrie that some players in the past, and even some managers, have felt haunted by the 1983 team. Not me. I am proud to be associated with a club which has such a rich European heritage and which produced such a wonderful side. You cannot be intimidated by what has gone before, but we must all strive to live up to the standards set during the glory days at Pittodrie. That type of success may never be repeated, but it shouldn't stop us from trying and it can certainly never be seen as a millstone around our necks. We have to aim to create our own piece of history, to be up there on the walls alongside the great players and managers of the past."

When Calderwood joined the Dons in 2004 he passed up the opportunity to lead Dunfermline, the club he left behind, into Europe having secured qualification with the Pars. It was a big decision for the former Birmingham player, who had never before sampled continental competition despite a distinguished managerial career in the Netherlands and more recently Scotland. He had to be patient but the big chance did eventually materialise and he soaked up every last drop of the Uefa Cup essence when he proudly led out Aberdeen against Dnipro on home turf in front of an expectant audience in September 2007.

Calderwood said: "I waited many years for my first taste of European football and it left me with a hunger for more. I am always excited before a game, but it was different. The whole city came alive in the build-up to the Dnipro tie. Even although we have been playing poorly and have suffered some bad results there were only positive vibes from all quarters. It was a big occasion from a personal point of view and I had my family up for the game including my sister, brother-in-law and nephews. We went out for a pre-match meal and everybody we encountered was so excited about what lay ahead, it was unique. I loved the whole experience and was immensely proud of what our players did on the night. Having experienced European nights at Pittodrie, when the atmosphere is simply fantastic, I'm desperate to earn some more. As I know from my own experience, and as I have told the players in no uncertain terms, these chances don't come along too often. We all have to make sure we seize the moment."

For chairman Stewart Milne the renaissance on the field has eased the burden of leading the club. He has gradually been able to withdraw from the frontline having steadied the ship after a particularly turbulent period and is confident the club is on a firm footing on all levels. Milne has endured some torrid times at recent annual meetings but the 2007 agm, amid the excitement of the Uefa Cup run, provided a welcome relief and was attended by a largely content group of shareholders.

Milne told the meeting: "My commitment to Aberdeen is as great now as it has ever been but I have to be realistic about the amount of time I can give to the club and I think very few people appreciate what goes into running a football club these days. You cannot do it on a part-time basis and I would like to think we have structured the club in a way which is very solid. We have Willie Miller taking responsibility for the football side of things and Duncan Fraser, as managing director, taking charge of the business side of the club. The structure is there and I can be more objective in a role operating in the background, to be a sounding board if they are needed."

Just as his illustrious predecessor Dick Donald found, success, albeit relative in the modern era, comes at a price. The return to Europe created its own set of problems as contract negotiations with the management team and bulk of the first team loomed. Just as Donald faced a fight to keep the Gothenburg team together, the current Dons regime must work hard to maintain the momentum which built under Calderwood.

Milne said: "There is no guarantee we will be able to keep all the players who are free agents at the end of the season, but Jimmy and Willie are working very hard and there are very good packages on the table for them. I would say we are optimistic most of them will stay and, hopefully, we will be able to persuade the manager to stay on as well. We have always said to Jimmy if he delivers success he is going to be noticed and if there are opportunities which he thinks are better for him then we will sit down and discuss them with him."

One of the key concerns for Calderwood during those negotiations over his own deal was the scope for continuing to improve the squad he shaped during his first three years in charge. The Uefa Cup experience of 2007/08, coupled with the income from Russell Anderson's £1million transfer to Sunderland, enabled the board to direct an additional £1.4million to the football budget over three years. That investment did come with a warning for the Red Army from the chairman, on the back of disappointing early season gates for domestic games despite the healthy crowds for the Uefa Cup action which included sell-outs.

Milne said: "It's a comfort the shareholders in general can see progress is being made - but we would feel a lot happier if more fans were coming to Pittodrie on a regular basis. We thought finishing third in the SPL in 2007 and making it back into Europe would be a major turning point for the club. It was hoped the crowds would start to grow a bit. But instead they have dropped and that is alarming. We want to build on what has happened, but if we don't get more support from the fans we could start to slide backwards again. Keeping a team able to get into and compete at European level costs money. It's hard enough as it is trying to persuade players to come here when they know there is a lot more money on offer to them in England. We are doing our best, but the investment in the team has to be reflected by the number of people turning up to games."

Where those people will be turning up to games could prove to be one of the most important factors in shaping the future of the club. If the plans for a new community stadium in time for the 2011/12 season come to fruition and the Pittodrie site can be sold, the financial situation would improve overnight. It could bring the Dons back to square one and to the longed for days when the black cloud of debt and financial worries did not hover over the club. Then the pace of the rebuilding can be increased, the future can be relished and the glory days can return.

The dream lives on.